GLORIA VANDERBILT BOOK OF
COLLAGE

FLOWERS WITH WALLPAPER

GLORIA VANDERBILT BOOK OF
COLLAGE

Gloria Vanderbilt
with Alfred Allan Lewis

GALAHAD BOOKS • NEW YORK CITY

Color photographs by Malcolm Varon, New York

Black and white photographs by Paul Jensen

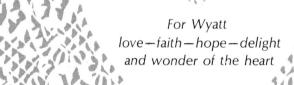

For Wyatt
love—faith—hope—delight
and wonder of the heart

Designed by Jean Callan King

Copyright © 1970 by Litton Educational Publishing, Inc.
Library of Congress Catalog Card Number 73-87039
ISBN: 0-88365-097-5

CONTENTS

FOREWORD

By Wyatt Cooper

Artists are different from you and me. They see more, for one thing. They dig deep. They feel more acutely. An artist is a brave and foolish creature of extraordinary p[er]ception and overwhelming response, and there's not much he can do about it. He [is] struck dumb by things that we pass by without a glance. He is filled with reverence [at] the sight of the light passing through the green of a tree, and he can trace the rivers [of] time in the veins of a leaf. He finds all spectacle in the smallest flower and all simplic[ity] in the sunset. He sees divinity in a passing ant and eternity in a moment. He knows t[he] sweetness that is in the clouds and the music that is in the lightning. Sky, land, mou[n]tains, rivers, all are his because he perceives them best. He is a part of everything th[at] grows, of all water that flows; he is reborn with every birth and he dies with eve[ry] death. The artist is consumed by a greed for life, and life rewards his devotion w[ith] grandeur and with pain. It rewards him with agonies and with revelations that the r[est] of us know not of. He is on intimate terms with the universe and he moves to its o[wn] strange, sad, and majestic harmony. He hears the sound of all humanity in a sin[gle] laugh remembered, and he can enfold all mankind in the stroke of one arm. He si[ngs] of what is unknown; he celebrates that which is unknowable; and what is not he ho[lds] in the palm of his hand. He is all hunger and passion, feeding on mystery. He lives [in] fractures of a vision, and he survives on the capture of transient moments. He is co[m]pelled to try to give form and permanence to what is formless, impermanent, a[nd] eternally elusive. He is compelled to define the undefinable, translate the untransl[at]able, and explain the inexplicable. He struggles on from failure to failure, all lust a[nd] fire and anger and soul and sensation, always searching after some siren song of t[he] spheres, forever feeling about for the pulse of the earth, and now and then he will [hit] some little something that is just a bit, in part at least, not totally removed from w[hat] he'd hoped for.

It may be true that the artist is unlike you and me. Or it may be that he is *just li[ke]* you and me, only more so.

Of course they're like us only more so! The artist, like the rest of us, spends his da[ys] precariously teetering on a tightrope, blindly plunging along, always in danger of tu[m]bling off into absurdity, and never quite certain whether truth or even logic waits at t[he] other end.

What we are talking about is awareness—our awareness of the human drama, of the glory and miracle and irony and comedy of it, and we have all had that awareness in one degree or another for some thousands of years now.

We are talking about that part of man's makeup that is reckless and restless and fanciful; that part of man that dreams and invents, plots and plays, and draws and decorates. It is exactly that divine madness in man that marks him as a relative of the gods. What the serpent promised Eve came true, after all; when she ate of the Tree of Knowledge, man acquired that godlike wisdom and sensibility that has blessed and plagued him ever after. He discovered beauty and ugliness and he created Art. Since the day of the Fall, or since he came down from the trees, if you prefer a more prosaic version of our history, man has occupied himself, not only with the drudgery and sweating of the brow necessary for survival, but also with song and dance and pictures, all expressive of his delights and his sorrows; he has tried, through music and words and images, to communicate something of his hopes for living and his fears of oblivion. He wrestles with the awful knowledge that he must die, and he seeks to embellish the span of life that has been allotted to him with whatever has joy and meaning: The artist, more than anyone, gives himself over to the pursuit of some kind of visual form that shows us the nobility of mind and ferocity of spirit that is timeless and eternal in the race of man; he stakes out man's small claim to the only kind of immortality we know of, even as he seeks to preserve whatever is unique in himself, so that something of his own individual personality should survive.

It is, I should think, to those dual efforts that we respond in an artist's work; we respond to that which is universal about it, in that it expresses a larger truth about man, and we respond to that which is personal, in that it tells us something about the artist himself—how he views the world about him, and how he feels about what he sees.

I say "Thank God" for artists. They are the better part of ourselves. We look at what they have done and we say, "Ah, I recognize that! It is precisely what I would have done if I'd had the tools, the skill, and the art to give form to my feelings." The artist shows us logic and meaning in the world where we see only confusion and disorder. He maintains his sanity by taking bits and pieces of the chaos around him and molding it into something that has balance and order and coherence for him. We look at the result and our own sanity is preserved. In showing us what he sees, the artist teaches us *how* to see. We take another look at what is familiar and we discover what we missed before.

Small wonder, then, that we cherish the artist, for we admire in him what we admire in ourselves. We like in him what we like in ourselves. In J. D. Salinger's *Catcher in the Rye*, Holden Caulfield, that astute critic of the modes and manners of his times, makes the following observation: "What really knocks me out is a book that, when you're all done reading it, you wish the author that wrote it was a terrific friend of yours and you could call him up on the phone whenever you felt like it." I think that's a pretty good way to feel about books and the authors that wrote them, and I don't see why it shouldn't apply as well to paintings and the painters that painted them. I, myself, would love to be able to get Fra Angelico on the phone whenever I felt like it—and Michelangelo and Picasso and Andrew Wyeth while we're at it; it would be nice to call up and invite them all over for coffee and a chat some afternoon. Also Grandma Moses. Most anybody who has ever looked at one of her enchanted paintings must have felt as I have felt, that it would be awfully refreshing to drop by her farmhouse and sit a spell. Furthermore, if you're like me, you felt that you knew what to expect; you could imagine the voice, the laugh, the straight, simple talk, the shrewd, honest humor of the eyes—even the cooking; you knew it all already, or felt as if you did.

And that's why, though it might be pleasant to get acquainted with folks of that ilk, though it might be fun to be on a first name, let's-pop-around-the-corner-to-the-movies basis with Leonardo, Rembrandt, Hieronymus Bosch, and the like, it's not really necessary, because you already know them through their art. If something in the painting touches you deeply, then you probably have a good idea of the person who created it, or at least of some aspect of him, and a personal encounter is likely to add little to what the work has already given you.

In bringing together any such assemblage of artists as the above, I would certainly want to include Gloria Vanderbilt in the group. It does happen, of course, since she is my wife, that I have some inside knowledge of the sunlight that her presence would add to the gathering. True, I have some acquaintance with that lady's charm of manner, beauty of person, and sweetness of disposition; but even if I did not, even if I had only of late come fresh upon her paintings, I'm certain that I should respond to them as I do now, and that I would have every desire in the world to call her up.

Mind, I do not claim that I view her work in a detached and objective way. I don't view *any* work in a detached and objective way. I don't even believe in being detached and objective. Lord, deliver us all from objectivity and detachment. Leave that for those serious-minded persons who regard themselves and their views with a ponderous solemnity. Leave it for certain persons who are not so much interested in knowing what they are thinking as in knowing what they ought to be thinking. I am interested in my feelings, if you want to know what I'm interested in. Whoever invented that old cliché, "I don't know anything about art but I know what I like," was probably wiser than he's given credit for. It's so much better than knowing all about art and *not* knowing what you like, and it's getting harder every day to know what one likes. The thing about art, surely, is the response—that's what the fellow had in mind when he picked up his brush in the first place; the work needs to be enjoyed, and one of the happy things about Gloria Vanderbilt's pictures is that unless you've long ago hardened your heart, it's almost impossible not to respond to them. Show me somebody who isn't made to feel better on looking at them, and I'll show you a grouch who hates Christmas. I wake up every morning in a room filled with her work, and you have my impartial word that they have a profound effect on my normally morose nature. After a few minutes with them I can turn to the obituaries in the *Times* with the most cheerful of hearts.

When people discover her pictures for the first time, there is usually some element of surprise in their reaction—surprise that the work is so personal, so individual, so open and without hesitation; they are surprised that so much is revealed. There's a bit of the shock of recognition; "Oh, so that's what she's like!" the stranger says. She has, it seems to me, arrived at that stage in the life of an artist when everything he does is uniquely his own, when the artist and his art can not be separated. To know one is to know the other. One senses that behind her canvases, there lives someone who takes a very special kind of delight in life, someone who can grasp a fantasy and give it breath, someone to whom the most unlikely of things can seem an everyday occurrence. One senses that there's somebody there who is real and sad and gay, somebody who believes in magic, probably, and certainly somebody who is intensely human and more than a little alive. She seems compelled to share something of her vision of life with the viewer, and he is invited to join her in her own extraordinary world. Her pictures reach out and embrace you. They are, in short, friendly. You are put at ease at first meeting. I think I'll call her Gloria.

Gloria's pictures cast a spell. They also ask that you pause and look at things anew. "Take a moment," they seem to say, "really to *see* this color, and that one, and the unexpected thing that happens when they're put next to each other. Look at the butterfly. See how simple it is. This is paper lace. Did you know that lace could do that? The flower is only a scrap of impossibly bright paper. The sky a yard of gingham. They're not disguised. They constantly remind you of what they are. Yet they add up to a world of pattern and play, of ribbons and fancy. In the bits and pieces, odds and ends, scraps and trifles that are everywhere around, she finds the stuff to build a dream of. Silver and gold and little pieces of the past are put together in a way that tells a story, evokes an essence, creates a mood, or simply asks us to look freshly at something that's worth looking freshly at. The pictures have tone and spirit and temper.

If you take the time and really give yourself over to the enjoyment of something that is pretty and sensuous and original and seductive, you may find that the work is more powerful than you at first suspected. It has backbone and marrow and a durability of construction that is no accident.

She used to do a lot of paintings of fragile-looking little girls plodding across pretty landscapes or playing with vivid balloons on a sugar-coated beach. They were charming, sweet, and touching, those little girls, and you were inclined to wax sentimental over them, murmuring "Bless their little hearts," a few times, until you began to be aware of the sturdiness of those little limbs, the steely determination in the thrust of the heads, the tough straightness of the backs, even the clean sweep of the long hair blowing in the breeze, and then you realized that, for all their delicacy and their wistful femininity, these were young ladies who knew exactly where they were going and what they were going to do when they got there. You could chuckle fondly over them if you liked, but if you were apprehensive for them, you were wasting your time.

The sap of life flows in the veins of those little girls; the wisdom of their race and the instincts of their sex are to be found in the hungry eyes that stare unblinkingly out t the world. She is romantic, this child of Gloria's creation; she holds a daisy in her and and she sighs for the stars, but lurking somewhere around the corners of her mouth and just behind the eyelashes is the knowledge that, taken for all and all, the moon is just another planet and it can be reached. Then there are those golden-haired nymphs gazing soulfully out at you from their garlands of flowers; they are full of the wonder of the universe; they exhale an air of perfumes and maidenly submission, but the longer you look the more it dawns on you that Little Miss knows all. She's onto the secrets of nature because she feels its mystery move in her own soul. She sits in quiet and listens to the music of her own heart.

Gloria's pictures lift the spirit. They communicate, and the message seems to get through to quite a lot of people. In 1966 she showed 120 paintings, mostly acrylics, at the Hammer Gallery in New York. The walls were blanketed with her pictures; the gallery seemed to vibrate with light and color, and the atmosphere of the place was unbelievable. For three weeks people streamed through; many came several times. "I'd forgotten you could go into a gallery and have a good time," I heard one lady say. It was gay and exciting, rather like one long party except that the intoxication came from what was on the walls, rather than from a bottle. To give that amount of pleasure in a world where most have forgotten even to expect pleasure—to create something that actually makes people feel better at a time when many no longer remember that there is any better to feel—well, I think she's a lucky girl, that's what I think.

She has been painting since she was a child and the funny thing is that the early ones—or, anyway, the ones we have that she did when she was 10—are immediately recognizable as hers. They aren't all that different, really, from what she does today. There is the same naiveté, the same sort of practical fantasy; but, then, there is something childlike in the work still, in her unabashed love of color, in the simplicity of the drawing, and in the directness of the vision. There is something of a paradox in her art, for it is curiously primitive and sophisticated at the same time. Though the pictures are refreshingly without guile and seem to be spontaneously conceived and set down, they are sometimes marvelously complex in execution. Though they are joyful and decorative, there is also a feeling of intense emotion held under control. Though they sing out in celebration of life, there is also a keen awareness of pain and sorrow. It may be that all joy is a victory over pain, and that an awareness of delight can not exist without an awareness of pain. The pictures often make me laugh, and in the laughter there is recognition that in the work good humor triumphs over bad, joy chides gently at despair. There is a delicate sort of self-awareness, of the artist's looking at her own seriousness of purpose with one eye cocked in self-amusement. The work is positive, optimistic, and vigorous. There is strength that comes a bit disguised, perhaps, that is startling when you notice it, rather like lilies made of iron.

Besides talent, skill, and inspiration, any artist, to succeed, must be capable of drudgery and he must have fantastic powers of concentration. Both of these Gloria has in abundance. When she is preparing for a show she works with such feverish intensity that unless I call her at the studio and remind her to eat, she is inclined to forget about it, and sometimes, unless I go after her, she will forget to come home. Recently, a friend of mine, speaking of a great surgeon, said, "He concentrates more completely than anybody I ever saw," and I realized that of course that must be true. It is true of great surgeons and it must be true of great artists. They must have the ability to exclude from their minds anything that would come between themselves and the task at hand.

Though Gloria's gifts are many, I should think that her greatest talents lie in her tremendous appetite for life, her quick response of delicate sensibility, her instinctive grasp of whatever is new or vital, her immense curiosity about all things, great or small, cosmic or trivial, her willingness to face experience, her openness to change, and her restless quest for perfection in every detail of living. She moves on strange planes, that girl; she is a creature of some mystery, not altogether of this world, part wood nymph, part Earth Mother, and part American Beauty Rose. She has the freshness of Snow White and the glamour of the Wicked Queen. She is as exotic as a unicorn and as subtle as an Egyptian temple cat. She is as crisp as gingham, as sensuous as satin, and as inscrutable as velvet. She is also as tentative as a doe in the forest, as delicate as a spider's web, as glittering as frost on a windowpane, and as pliant as a willow. She is as gay as a meadowlark, as clean as a day in the country, as cool as strawberries, and as healthy as a pitcher of milk. "She walks in beauty like the night" (Byron) and if she has not yet made of herself a living work of art, she's come damned close, or as close as anybody I'd ever want to meet.

INTRODUCTION

Most painters, at one time or another, work in collage. Braque has; so has Picasso. So have children in school even before they start finger painting. Chances are you've made collages every day without knowing it. For arranging things is a form of collage. Whether it is a group of pictures on the top of a piano, or ashtrays, flowers, and books on a table top, or even garden vegetables on a kitchen table—you are unknowingly exercising the impulses you would follow in making a collage. Whenever a woman suddenly gets a certain look in her eye, jumps up and dashes over to a table to rearrange, perhaps for the thousandth time, the objects displayed there, so that they have some new relationship that pleases her, it may seem like puttering to her husband—but to those who know, she's really making a table top collage.

I came upon collage quite by accident, but it was only after I'd been working in it for some time that I realized how closely connected the everyday activity of arranging and rearranging things is to the artist's constant search for new forms in which to find expression. Collage is a natural medium for all people who enjoy their family, their house, and ways of expressing their own individuality.

My work table is an old drafting table with lots of shallow drawers in which I store the bits and pieces I intend to use in my work—things like old and new photographs, postcards, valentines and greeting cards, paper dolls, lace doilies, aluminum foil, lengths of fabric, and myriad other things. The top isn't usually arranged so neatly: I have put out my tools and some of the fabrics I might use in a collage. If you look carefully, you'll find tweezers, scissors, a razor blade, a mat knife, glue, an iron, paint brushes, tubes of acrylic paint, and a gesso board.

Detail of ALSATIAN GIRL

My first collage started with a paper lace mat. I'd always been drawn to lace, and one day I came across this doily which had been lying around my studio. I don't even remember how it got there. I've always collected things, and this probably caught my eye because there was something interesting in the texture of the paper so delicately worked into a Valenciennes pattern. It turned up under a pile of magazines I was looking through at a time when I was starting to work on a drawing of an Alsatian girl with a lace headpiece and collar. I related the lace to the sketch immediately and just for amusement cut the lace into appropriate shapes and put it over the head of my drawing and under her chin. It was fascinating. A whole new world of possibilities opened up. Such a moment brings flashes of insights. You suddenly know what you want to do. When it happens, go with it. Ideas for pictures that I wanted to do came crowding into my head. Tens upon tens of them. So many that I knew I wouldn't be able to do them all. In any case, I knew marvelous things were about to happen. They did, and it was for me the beginning of a delicious, rewarding, and fulfilling adventure. It can be for you too. And that, I hope, is what this book is all about.

ALSATIAN GIRL

There's nothing really new about collage. The Victorians made all sorts of pretty pictures with pressed leaves and dried flowers and cutout figures. Your mother probably cut out flowers from magazines and glued them onto boxes and then lacquered them, which is a process called decoupage.

As I am often asked the difference between decoupage and collage, this seems as good a place as any to give you my dictionary's definition of the two words:

Decoupage—"the art, technique, or method of decorating something with paper cutouts. . . ."

Collage—"a technique of composing a work of art by pasting on a single surface various materials not normally associated with one another, as newspaper clippings, theater tickets, fragments of an envelope, etc. . . ."

Don't let yourself be intimidated by that "work of art" in the definition. In the hands of Picasso a collage can become a great work of art, but that's not for us to worry about. Let's enjoy ourselves. Collage is a simple and exciting form of creative expression. Anybody can do it. If you think of the delight that you are given by the primitive collages children bring home from school, and if you decide that in your own efforts you will merely do the same things with a little more sophistication, then you should be able to proceed without fear of failure.

Besides being fun and satisfying, collage is also marvelously inexpensive. You don't need to make a big investment in elaborate equipment. Everybody has a fully equipped collage atelier without knowing it. Your kitchen can serve as your workshop. And as for tools and materials, to start all you really need is a good pair of scissors, the cardboard from a freshly laundered shirt (or the top of a department store box), glue or paper cement, some pieces of colored paper or fabric—these plus a sense of adventure, for it is an adventure you are embarking upon. Once you get into it, you find yourself looking at things in a new way. Everything becomes a possible element in a picture: soap wrappers, magazine illustrations and photographs, hair ribbons, gift paper, book jackets, greeting cards, pressed flowers, aluminum foil—almost anything. It actually is this easy to get started.

One thing I suggest is that in each picture you use at least one object that you really love. Everybody has an attic, a spare closet, a catch-all kitchen drawer, in which are stored all of the odd bits and pieces no longer useful but carefully tucked away because we haven't been able to bring ourselves to part with them.

The reason I stress using something you love is that your affection for it will probably influence the shape the picture ultimately takes. The form in which you put together the objects you like comes much more from your personal feelings than from any training in art. Also, it is your feelings that tell you when your picture is completed. This too is something that cannot be learned. No painting has a real finish that can be defined before the painter reaches it. If it's successful, it simply stops at a good place. This is especially true in collage. The picture tells you when to stop. You paste on one extra piece of paper lace, and it seems to say all by itself—that's it. Not another thing. I'm finished.

Before I begin to tell you about my collages, why not jump in feet first? Let's try a collage together. First of all, get some old newspaper and spread it over the kitchen table or floor. This will protect the work surface from any accidents with glue and make it easier to gather up snippets from your cutting.

Next, get your backing board. Any piece of cardboard with even edges will do nicely. My personal preference is gesso board, because I love the smooth texture of its surface and its whiteness, and it's a good stiff backing, but you probably don't have any in the house, and it's an unnecessary expense at this point, especially for the kind of picture we're going to do.

It's not necessary to use gesso, even if you want some white background to be exposed. Cardboard, plywood, or some other material (backing can be any-thing that is sufficiently stiff not to buckle under the weight of paste and ob-jects) can easily be painted white with house paint, deck paint—any white paint you have at hand. I prefer acrylic, because it holds the white and does not yellow with age. Apply a thin coat of the paint very carefully. Any lumpi-ness will show through whatever you paste over it. Moreover, thick patches are likely to turn into a sticky mess should you want to iron over them. In painting, this base coat is called a primer and the application of it, priming. It does not have to be white; you can prime in any color that strikes you as the right one for the background of your picture.

I like to work with barber's scissors, but any pair of household shears with a good cutting edge will do. Later, as you go along, you may want to experi-ment with different sizes and weights of scissors. When you hit upon the right one for you, you'll know it by the good heft it has in the hand. It will flow and wheel freely. The next item is some strong glue or paper cement. My usual choice is a spray-can variety because I find it the easiest to control, but you might choose Elmer's glue and a brush.

Now, just follow the steps shown in the pictures opposite and on the follow-ing pages.

1. All the materials necessary: a pair of scissors, a razor blade, some shiny black gift-wrapping paper, a roll of ordinary aluminum foil, a sheet of plain white paper, glue, and a backing board (you could substitute a piece of cardboard from a laundered shirt).

2. Put aside everything except for the backing board and the black gift paper.

3. Turn the gift paper over and place the backing board on top of it. If you have an evenly squared corner (the beginning or end of the roll), use it.

4. With the razor blade, cut the gift paper along the edge of the backing board so that you have a piece that will exactly cover the board. Then turn over the board so that the paper is on top.

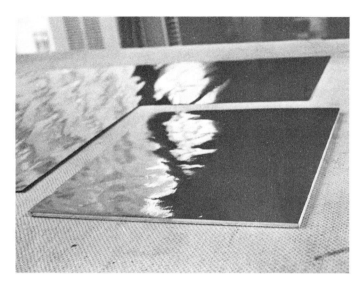

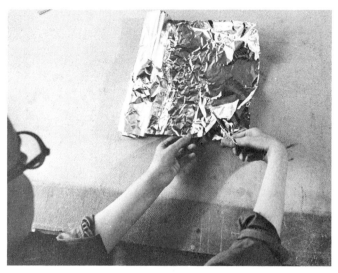

5. Paste the gift paper to the backing board so that the entire surface is neatly paved with the black paper. (The light areas on the paper in the photograph are reflections.)

6. Cut the shape of a vase directly from the aluminum foil.

7. Draw the simplest, most primitive flower on the white paper.

8. Leaving a nice margin, cut out the area on which you've sketched the flower.

9. Carefully cut around the flower with the scissors until all the excess is trimmed away from its outline.

10. Place the aluminum-foil vase on the black-surfaced backing board and move it around until you find a composition that pleases your eye.

11. Place the flower in the vase (you can move the shapes around some more if you change your mind about the arrangement at this point) and paste the pieces down. As a final touch, you might cut a small circle of black paper and paste it down to make the center of the white flower. And there is a finished collage. That's all there is to it!

There are dozens of variations you can make on this very simple collage—for instance, using a paper of the same shade as the dominant color of the room where you plan to hang the work and a flower cut from a scrap of upholstery fabric. Or you might add some other shapes—you will be surprised to find how one simple collage can draw you into trying others.

The rest of this book is devoted to some of the more complicated and advanced techniques of collage. There's nothing to fear in attempting any of them. All they require is a sense of adventure and materials almost as rudimentary as the ones you've just used—things you've been looking at for a lifetime, things that, with a slight adjustment of vision, can be seen in the new light of this exciting medium. Collage can be the most personal, amusing, satisfying, and immediate of art forms. In it you can create an exotic and special world out of the most ordinary objects.

CHAPTER ONE

Once I tuned into the extraordinary world of collage, all sorts of commonplace objects began to assume new meanings and to have myriad purposes. Kitchen shelves became laden with undreamed of possibilities. A bottle cap was not only a cover for soda, it was something that might be used in a picture. After all, Pop artists have shown us how to look at banal objects like soup cans and really see them for the first time. I had always been a collector, and now it was with special delight that I looked through boxes of old photographs, odd pieces of wallpaper and fabrics, wrapping from packages, ribbons, and old postcards. Textures, colors, shapes, postage stamps, greeting cards, and hundreds of other familiar things that you see every day suddenly have the possibility of magic. Your eye begins to see things in a new way. Looking around, I realized how many possibilities there were in things it would never have occurred to me to use. (At this very moment, I'm impatiently waiting for some Porthault sheets with blue and red flowers to wear out. The print will be marvelous in a future collage.)

Once you start collecting, family and friends will get caught up in your enthusiasm. Mine did, and soon they were bringing me objects that caught their eye. My five-year-old son Carter brought me the gold wrappings from some chocolate candy coins and said, "For a collage, Mommy," and I prized them, too.

I brought my whole collection together and started a file. It helps to be organized. A bookcase makes an excellent file, but if you don't have that much space to spare, you can use an old carton. It's a good idea to put a sheet of cardboard or paper between each group of pictures, postcards, box tops, labels, or whatever else you are accumulating. Don't think about the ultimate place in a specific collage for any of these things. As long as they please you, they'll eventually find their way into a picture.

GREEN FLOWERPOTS

Pictures start in many ways, and then the objects fall into place. One of m
early collages began with my reaction to color. I was looking through shee
of colored composition paper in an art supply store and the richness of th
colors thrilled me—I was astonished to see how many shades of each colc
one could buy. I was fascinated not only by the subtle variations of each shad
but by what happens when you put one color next to another. I couldn't wa
to start discovering where these extraordinary colors would lead.

In my studio I had a gesso board that measured 36 by 24 inches. I'd bee
planning to do a painting on it but decided instead to use it as the backing fc
this collage, which became "Green Flowerpots" (page 19).

The sky blue, magenta, and purple papers were so right together that the
cried out to be the background. I cut them into rectangles and covered th
bottom third of the board with purple, two-thirds of the remainder with blue
and the rest with magenta. Don't ask how I hit upon this equation, because
don't know. It simply looked right, and so it was right. Before gluing, I pu
the picture on the floor to study the effect of the colors in combination. Some
thing was wrong. The blue jarred when bordering right on the other colors.
moved it a little, so that a ribbon of white gesso showed through, isolating
from its neighbors. The white gave the colors boldness and vitality. I spraye
a thin layer of paste over the back of the papers and then pressed them dow
carefully so that the corners met the corners of the gesso board. To make ce
tain the collage would not buckle, I covered it with a clean sheet of paper an
piled books on it.

After that, I cut samples from the other sheets and moved them aroun
against the background before selecting the next shade. I liked a chartreuse
started cutting into it, and let the scissors wander. Out of this grew an abstrac
tion of a flowerpot. When I put the flowerpot on the picture, the purpl
became a table against a magenta wall, and the blue became a window ope
to the sky.

Despite my background in painting, it never occurred to me to draw a rea
istic flowerpot on the chartreuse paper. I did not want to do any drawing a
such. I let the scissors replace the pen. All in one piece, the silhouette of th
pot emerged and then the stem and leaves and flower of the plant.

It is almost impossible to explain the creative process in this, or, for tha
matter, any other piece of work. What I can express is the importance of work
ing out of the subconscious, which is one of the fundamental joys of collage
Try not to think. Thinking may interrupt your instinct and your natural creativ
flow. Trust your impulse and your head—knowing that, with a little bit c
luck, each will temper the other. Wield the scissors with a free hand and you
intent will very often come through with surprising results. Once, when Jea
Cocteau visited Isadora Duncan and tried to do a drawing of her, he aban
doned the pen for scissors and started cutting out shapes from paper. Th
unused snippings scattered to the floor. Glancing down, he was astonishe
to see in one of the discarded pieces a startling likeness to the dancer. It wa
his most successful portrait. Arrived at quite by chance? Not really, for his im
pulse and creative intent was behind every twist and turn of his wrist. It alway
is. Work out of your subconscious, and the essence of your initial impulse an
point of view will follow through. At this point you might say, "But suppos
I have no creative impulse?" I don't believe it. I think all of us do. Certainl

all children do—only, alas, it's very often diverted into more realistic channels somewhere along the line. But I suspect that it's still there in all of us, waiting to be rediscovered.

I cut two more chartreuse pots of different sizes and moved all three around against the background. No matter how I placed them in relationship to one another, the composition retained an air of austerity. There was not enough color or clutter. More objects were necessary. Out of a deeper shade of green, I cut a fourth pot. A lavender caught my eye and I thought—why not a perfume bottle?

I interrupt the explanation of "Green Flowerpots" again here because it occurs to me that I seem to contradict myself by outlining an intellectual thought process when I have just told you to try not to think. For the sake of clarity, in this book I will often outline such thought processes—but they may or may not have occurred in the manner I remember.

The perfume vial was no more realistic than the flowerpots, but that didn't bother me at all. All pictures are essentially abstract, even a Gainsborough portrait. It's a question of the degree of abstraction, and that's up to the vision of the individual artist.

The next object to emerge was a bright red tray. Red is the most forceful color for accent: it makes everything around it seem much more alive. Again I scrambled the cut pieces and tried out countless relationships. It is astonishing to see the number of compositions that can be assembled from the same few elements.

When I found the right places for the flowerpots, the picture still seemed to need more color and texture: the green flowers should bloom. I decided to try introducing a new element—fabric. I carefully cut out discs of a red and white checked linen. But the care with which I cut defeated my purpose. The pieces were rigid, and the quality I loved most about collage was its fluidity. I tried again, this time using the scissors very freely, so that the material was more shredded than cut. Actually, I was allowing the tensile strength of the fabric fibers to dictate the path of the blade. The result had exactly the looseness I wanted. It was a circle without being a precise geometric form.

SHREDDING

Often, cutting fabrics with a hard edge makes them seem of a too predetermined pattern, as if turned out by a cookie cutter. I sometimes seek to avoid this by shredding, which leaves an irregular edge that strikes me as having more life. In shredding, I use the scissors as an edge along which to pull the fabric in the general shape I want to obtain. However, there are many other ways to cut out pieces for collage, depending on the effect you want. Two other techniques are illustrated on the following pages.

DECOUPAGE

This is a very delicate, precise technique of cutting out patterns.
Above, left: The print from which I want to cut flowers, stem, and leaves.
Above, right: I carefully cut around the edges of the subject with a scissors.
Below: For the fine interior portions of the design and the intricate edges, I use a razor to eliminate the unwanted areas.

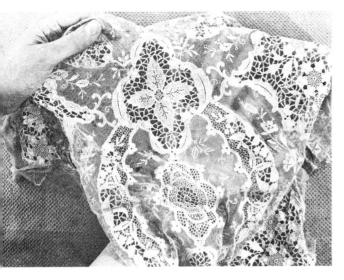
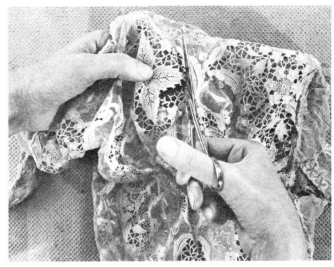

ACE PATTERNS

I often use designs cut from lace, both real (as shown here) and paper.
Above, left: The lace from which I want to cut the flower.
Above, right: With scissors, I snip the lace flower free from the surrounding threads.
Below: The result is a lace design that has a life of its own completely separated from
the original fabric.

Within the red and white circles I placed smaller circles of a tiny black and white gingham, again using the shredding technique of cutting. The result was blossoms that seemed to move instead of being stiffly formal. I thought that it might be amusing to give life to the scene by adding a butterfly and, accordingly, cut one out of the gingham. I scrambled the elements again, and the butterfly landed on the vial.

Only one thing still did not sit right in the composition. The red tray was such a bright color that it dominated any area in which it was placed. I did not want to eliminate it, because I liked the way the shade balanced the red in the flowers. Looking around for another solution, I found Carter's gold candy wrappings and placed them on the tray. Then, to bring the lavender of the bottle down to this part of the picture, I cut a small disc out of it and set it alongside the coins.

I pasted the pieces in place and piled books on the collage to flatten it. When I removed the weights, I found that they had flattened everything sufficiently except the fabric. I took a pressing iron and, to prevent scorching, I placed a cloth over the picture and ironed over that.

Again I studied the picture and again something struck me as wrong. The ribbon of exposed gesso overwhelmed everything else. At first I thought of pasting paper over it, but that would mean pulling up some of the pots and the vial. I decided to paint it out. Using acrylic paint of a magenta shade as close as possible to the color of the paper, I lightly brushed in the ribbons of white. The result was good. The ribbons still separated the areas of magenta and blue but more subtly—with a textural rather than a tonal barrier. The freedom of the medium enables one to incorporate almost anything into it.

Detail of GREEN FLOWERPOTS

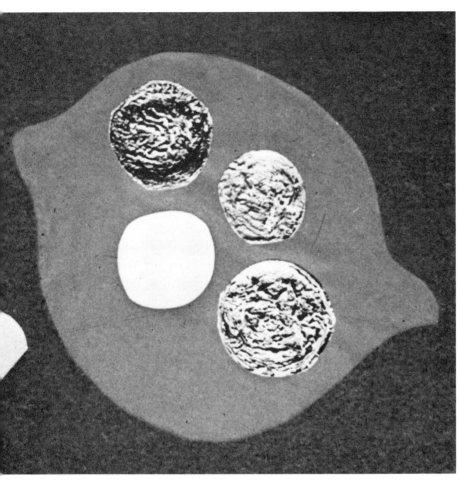

Detail of GREEN FLOWERPOTS

One advantage collage has over painting is that paint, once it is down on canvas, is there to stay unless you go through a laborious process of eradication or painting over; you can change your mind often and easily in collage. Just don't be in a hurry to paste. Give yourself a chance to move things around. Even when everything seems perfect, take time to look at it again. You can get so delighted with a particular effect that you lose sight of the total work.

Working with colored papers stimulated me into doing "Green Flowerpots." It's a strong color statement with a tonal balance that I feel good about because it's just what I meant. It's not often you can say that about a piece of work.

One successful picture leads to another. When I start working in one particular way, I like to continue until I've exhausted the subject. I did quite a number of variations on the flowerpot theme, using different shapes, sizes, and colors, before I left it. And even then, the subject cropped up again.

We have three aquariums at our house, and a fish tank seemed like an amusing subject. Fishes have streamlined shapes that naturally lend themselves to a certain amount of abstraction.

For "Fishes and Objects" (page 29), I chose a gesso board measuring 30 by 24 inches. I cut a large piece of pale green paper in a shape that was an impression of a fish tank. For the table, I used a still paler green, because I felt it had to be subordinate in tone to the dominant area. I left a lot of the gesso exposed, and a blue rectangle completed the colors in the background.

The fishes came next. I cut them out of shades of gray, pink, orange, red, and magenta, and pushed them around into various positions until they happened in a combination I liked. Then I added the air bubbles. When the time came for pasting these little pieces down, I discovered that one has to take great care. A steady spray made them curl over themselves; glue got on the surface and it was difficult to paste them down properly. The best way to handle very little pieces, I have discovered, is to apply a quick jab of spray or a small dab of whatever other paste you may use.

It remained to find the shapes that should be on the table. They turned out to be familiar ones—some of those I had worked with in "Green Flowerpots."

I cut out two pots, one green and the other yellow. For their centers, I decided on two ginghams, a tiny black and white check and a larger brown and white check. I again shredded rather than cut in roughly circular shapes. Because they had to hold their own against the powerful colors of the fish, I tried to draw some visual attention to them by placing black on brown in one flower and reversing the order in the other. The result was somewhat whimsical, which added to the lightness of the whole collage.

In preparing the perfume vial, I cut out the butterfly as part of the whole. The shape was actually not unrelated to the shape of the fishes. But in scrambling the elements, I discovered that the dark purple color was a little heavy. I considered putting the shape aside for another picture and using a lighter shade to make a new vial. But that would have disturbed the balance of color. The picture needed the somber note of the dark purple. The problem was how to lighten the effect of it so that it would harmonize with the happy mood of the rest of the composition. Out of lavender and white gingham I cut a butterfly, which I placed on the vial as a stopper. Not only did it brighten the tone of the bottle, but it added an interesting texture to the paper fishes.

Something structural was needed to balance and unify the composition. I scrambled many elements around before finally deciding on gingham mats and more of Carter's gold candy wrappers.

When you like certain shapes and fabrics, don't hesitate to use them over and over again. They become something different in each picture, because they have different functions in each. The important thing is to love something and not to worry about having used it before. If you really enjoy a shape or fabric or object, it will find its own new purpose each time out.

I like fishes and I did a series of collages with fishes in them. Each new version seems to have its own life. Artists often return time and again to one subject and find they always have something fresh to say about it.

I made "Table Setting" (page 29) to hang in the dining room of our house in Southampton. I worked on a 24-inch-square gesso. Since the materials and many of the objects were the same as those with which I had been working, the construction followed the same course as in the collages we've already discussed. I mention "Table Setting" here because one of the pleasures of doing pictures for your own use is that you can plan them to fit a place you've decided on and use fabrics and wallpaper already in the room. The result is something unique and personal. Just as you are especially proud of the bookcase your son built, and just as flowers grown in your own garden seem to have a special sweetness, you and your family are likely to get extra enjoyment from this kind of collage.

Earlier I told you that as you work in collage you will become more and more aware of the endless possibilities of all kinds of materials. You have no idea how many varieties of paper alone you can discover. With much more than passing interest, you will rummage through gift shops, novelty stores, five-and-ten-cent stores, stationers, all of the places where paper products are sold. You will find white and colored and gold and silver paper lace in countless patterns. There are companies that specialize in manufacturing paper frames and ribbons for people who like to make their own greeting cards. These things are not difficult to find and, what's more, they're inexpensive. I maintain a collection that serves me well in every collage I do.

Then there are greeting cards. Some contemporary ones are exciting, but even better are the old ones our parents and grandparents used to collect in albums. If searching the attic doesn't turn some up, try the local antique shops. This sounds as if it might cost a lot but it really doesn't. Many shops have boxes filled with old postcards, valentines, and photographs. I especially like old family photographs with pictures of children in lacy dresses and adults stiffly posed. Mrs. Caroline Guth from the Antique Box in New York City gave me dozens of wonderful ones taken from old albums she had for sale.

I also like to collect old valentines. There was one that I particularly liked, with a message that said, "Think of me." This brings me to "Think of Me" (page 29).

What I wanted to do was to re-create the kind of decorative clutter typical of the Victorian period. My use of flowerpots, perfume vials, and butterflies was certainly more extensive than in earlier pieces, but the process was the same. The backing was done in violet and three shades of yellow paper on a

Detail of THINK OF ME

gesso board measuring 24½ by 37 inches. I left lots of gesso showing, because I wanted the background kept fresh and clean. The colors were right for a memory piece: bright, but with a faded quality, as if the picture had been done long ago.

Later, the paper was to buckle slightly, probably because of the dampness at the beach. Strangely enough, the effect added to the feeling of aging and nostalgia. That brings up another bit of advice that is good to remember. Accidents and mistakes are not always as fatal as they at first seem. They sometimes work to your advantage by lending still another texture to your picture.

In doing the flowers, butterflies, and mats, I used a combination of eight different checked fabrics. Some, like the butterflies, were cut very precisely. I shredded others to give variety of form and texture.

The mirror on the wall faced directly out at the viewer. It is made of a plastic silver paper in which one can actually see a reflection. The mirror on the table was facing a different direction; it seemed only logical to use a different material. I cut out the center of a silver paper mat. A white paper lace place mat served for the cloth on the dressing table. All three materials are the sort easily found in any housewares store.

For the flowers in the small vases, I used decoupage. Decoupage is actually very simple. All you do is cut out the object you want to use, keeping as precisely to the edges as a child would in cutting out clothes for a paper doll.

Once the picture was under way, the need for one thing after another came naturally—comb, scissors, coins, the little gold tray, beads—assorted possessions that might be found on the dressing table of a girl at the turn of the century.

The strip of exposed gesso running vertically down the picture struck me as too strong, as needing something to soften it. I could have corrected this by painting over in another color, as I did in "Green Flowerpots," or by pasting on more colored paper. But instead, I introduced an entirely new material—a piece of ribbon embroidered with violet flowers. It had a nineteenth-century feeling about it, and I inserted it along the border separating the lavender from one of the yellow papers. It not only worked from a compositional point of view but also contributed to the period feeling.

There were so many objects in this picture that I rearranged them constantly in search of the right composition. If I'd pasted everything down immediately, I would never have been able to experiment with various juxtapositions.

It is fascinating to see how many compositions can emerge from precisely the same elements. The one I finally settled on was the one that pleased my eye the most, but any of a number of the others might have done equally well.

Looking at the completed picture, I felt it still needed a final object to tie it together. As it was now, it seemed to fall into two separate halves. I wanted something to unify it. I cut a pink and white gingham butterfly and placed it among the flowers in the top half of the picture, paralleling the angle of the valentine envelope. The lines of the two small, slightly askew objects had an inner tensile strength sufficient to bring together the many elements of a complicated canvas.

I love surprise in anything, and "Think of Me" achieves this. It started out with a Victorian valentine but, once under way, took on a life of its own. The final result is not a period piece at all, but unexpectedly of today.

Detail of THINK OF ME

THINK OF ME

FISHES AND OBJECTS

TABLE SETTING

FRUIT IN YELLOW BOWL by Mary R. Wilson

Inspiration for collages can come from many places. One of the richest sources is painting. Above is a work I particularly like, which I decided to reinterpret in terms of collage, using my favorite fabrics and colored paper—the materials assembled in the picture below. The process of making the collage was the usual: backing, scrambling the elements, and pasting them down. But the delicate stems in the painting led me to try a new material—copper wire—which I added as illustrated on the opposite page.

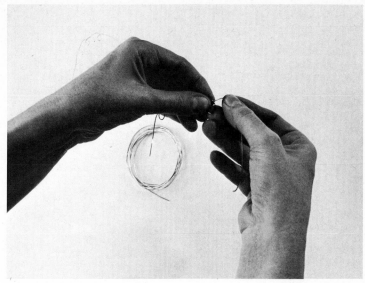

Above, left: I cut short lengths of thin copper wire from the five- and ten-cent store.

Above, right: I made loops of the wire to form curling tendrils.

Below: The finished collage. Attaching the wires to the collage was easy: I simply sewed them to the fabric backing with needle and thread, making the stitches at the underside of the curled wire so that they were inconspicuous.

THE MOTHER

CONSTANCY

CHAPTER TWO

I've always liked Victorian things. They have fantasy, sweetness, innocence, and imagination. They are ornate and decorative. I like to drop into antique shops, old print shops, curio shops, even thrift shops, and pick up odds and ends, bits and pieces of the clutter that marked that era. It was a natural step to build collages around such memorabilia and it was satisfying to find this way of displaying them so that they could give pleasure instead of being tucked away in a drawer.

"The Mother" (opposite) began when I came across the photograph of a marvelous grim-faced Victorian lady. The picture amused me and I began to build around it a world of pink paper and white lace curtains. It has been said of this collage that it makes a comment on the prettiness of the period and the iron butterflies who dominated it. And I suppose it does. What I had in mind was to contrast the severity of the face with something gay and light and feminine. Usually in starting a collage you will be inspired by one particular thing. Anything can be a starting point, and if you go with it all sorts of un- planned and often delicious things can happen. As the collage builds, and things are added to it, the process may take on a life of its own and, very often, lead you into unexpected places, so that when the work is finished it will be perhaps only a small fragment of your original intent. In the same way, you may be surprised by what other people sometimes think your work is about. Often, a work will quite legitimately suggest to one person something that seems far from what you intended. Don't be dismayed by this. Other interpre- tations can be quite valid and often give us insights into our own creative process.

Detail of THE MOTHER

For "The Mother," I started with a gesso board measuring 30 by 24 inches. After laying in the background, I indicated the curtain by running a border of white eyelet along the top and sides of the picture. Along the very top, I used an overlay of an edging with a delicate green embroidery. It not only served to bring the green to the top of the picture but also gave the illusion of a cornice or shade. It also evoked the femininity of the era. (This sort of edging can be picked up very inexpensively at five- and ten-cent stores, fabric shops, or the notions counter of any large department store.)

For the big flower, I used four different checks in shredded, layered circles. This kind of embellishment is not only great fun to do as an exercise in abstraction, but it also manages to convey a precise representational image. The leaves were cut from heavy green linen.

To offset the starkness of the photograph, I framed it in a bright ribbon and added the checked butterfly and colored marbles. To suggest that the room was lived in, I put in playing cards and coins. The butterfly at the top of the frame was a realistic one I had cut out from an old print. In connection with this I should mention that there is a shortcut that might be helpful to you. The actual work of cutting can be tedious and time-consuming. If you break the creative flow by stopping to do it, you can lose a great deal of momentum. What I do is cut in advance. If I come upon something that I think I might want to use in some future picture, I cut it out and put it aside. A perfect time to do this is of an evening while the family is watching television or while sitting under the dryer at the hairdresser's. I have even been known to snip out a few butterflies while waiting for a friend in a restaurant.

Another great time-saver is to keep your files full of materials. When you are inspired by one particular thing, you generally will not have to stop to look for other objects to complement it. More often than not, the elements I want to use are already on hand in my studio.

Fabric stores often advertise remnant sales. What a wonderful and inexpensive source of materials they are! At one of them, I found an absolutely enchanting piece of rose-point lace. It immediately suggested another Victorian collage.

For "Constancy" (page 32), I already had the charming old valentine and the envelope addressed to Miss Alice Cardwell of Norwich, Conn. The envelope was embossed and might well have once carried a similar card. They went beautifully with the lace.

I used a gesso measuring 20 by 24 inches and backed it with yellow and white and green and white ginghams. For the table, I selected a bright print of red and yellow flowers on a white field.

In pasting down background fabrics, I've discovered a way of almost completely avoiding the use of glue anywhere on the front, which might accidentally be stained. When cutting the fabric, I leave a healthy margin of about two inches beyond the edge of the backing board. I then flap this margin over the edge, pull it taut, and paste it firmly to the back of the board. In just about every instance, this is sufficient to hold the fabric in place without using any paste on the front. (This is illustrated on pages 94–95.) It is a good idea to press the fabric when you have finished.

Detail of CONSTANCY

I cut the vase out of a piece of old wallpaper and the bouquet from a length of flower-printed calico. To avoid rigidity of outline, I used the shredding technique.

The bold red and yellow of the table fabric overwhelmed the muted tones of everything else. To break it up, I used a delicately faded old piece of wallpaper as a mat on the table, and bits of orange calico and blue paper lace under the vase softened it still more. To carry the blue up and the turquoise of the bouquet down, I backed the lacy valentine with a rectangle of turquoise gingham just large enough to make a small border around it.

I cut flowers from the rose-point lace and scattered them over the calico. Around each, I left just enough net to soften the harsh edges. For variety—and because the wrong side of the lace was just as pretty as the front—I placed one lace flower back-side-front and let another drop to the orange gingham mat. The lacy bouquet echoed the lacy valentine delightfully. The ivory tones of the lace, the yellowing paper, and the cobweb filigree had the texture and delicacy of icing on a birthday cake.

I cut tiny red and magenta roses from a printed fabric and scattered them through the bouquet. Then I included a nineteenth-century certificate that I'd found at a local antique shop. One small lavender paper marble just beneath the valentine completed the highlighting colors.

I decided to border one side with lacy curtain-like edging. I'd found a broad ribbon of white with yellow eyelet embroidery, and I wanted to use a narrower ribbon with open work over it and let the yellow of the gingham background show through the openings in both patterns.

I pasted and ironed down the first ribbon. When I superimposed the second ribbon, the two patterns cancelled each other out, and all I got was solid white. The composition demanded that the yellow be brought over to the perimeter of the picture. This would have been accomplished if I used the broader ribbon alone, but it looked rather meager.

The solution proved to be a narrow yellow and white striped hair ribbon, which I sandwiched between the layers of edging. The yellow showed through the openings of the top tier and brought the color over to where I felt it had to be.

While I was searching for the hair ribbon, I came across a length of rick-rack embroidered with tiny yellow roses. I tried it out on the exposed portion of the broader edging and found that it just fitted inside the borders of the yellow embroidery and actually became a part of the overall design.

What had originally been intended to be the simplest of borders was actually composed of four separate parts. And it was exciting to do! This casting about for solutions to textural and tonal problems is wonderful. It is like solving a puzzle. A precision of design grows out of complete freedom of selection. It is extraordinary how small, seemingly random things can embellish and give new dimensions to a collage. If you feel the need for more, trust your instinct. Don't be afraid to let yourself go.

"Constancy" has a feeling of age that comes from the use of genuinely old and faded materials. If you want to simulate the same effect with brand new things, all you have to do is immerse them for a moment in cold coffee, and you have instant antique paper and lace.

Detail of CONSTANCY

Sometimes the most dissimilar things come together in the creation of a collage. That is what happened in "Red, White, and Blue" (opposite). In the notions department at a department store, I'd discovered a line of ribbons with a motif of national flags. Among those I bought was a red ribbon embroidered with British flags. This, surprisingly, was to come together with an old keepsake, a Brussels lace handkerchief that had belonged to my mother.

When I started the collage, I intended it to be no more than an exercise in stretching my color vocabulary. I love the combination of red, white, and blue, but had never worked with the colors until then. I wondered what would happen if I did a collage using only strong variations of them.

I decided to work in a small area and chose a gesso of 13½ by 9½ inches. I backed it with two shades of blue paper separated by a band of gesso. It seemed natural to add the red and white checked gingham tablecloth.

The color was vibrant, and I wanted to keep the small composition simple. I used aluminum foil for the vase. One large blossom was made of layers of red, white, and blue checked fabric and paper.

After moving the flower and vase around, I decided they looked best when completely backed by the darker blue panel. But something was needed to hold them down compositionally, or they looked too glaring. So I put a band of the Union Jack ribbon above the flower. The result was what I had aimed at—an unsentimental exercise in color—but I found it was not what I really wanted at all. Against the boldness of the darker side, the pale blue panel seemed washed out. The alternating hot and cold tones were *too* simply stated to suit my taste. I missed the human element and found it in an old French class certificate of merit. The figure of the boy was suitable, unsentimental, and straightforward, and his uniform suggested some connection with the ribbon flags.

To bring the two sections together, I cut two marbles out of the bold check in the flower. I set them over the certificate and topped it all with a red heart cut from a printed ribbon, leaving a small border of the white background intact. Then, to add texture, I placed the Brussels lace handkerchief as a mat under the vase. Its delicate strength held its own in a way that was both unexpected and interesting.

"Red, White, and Blue" now hangs in our children's nursery, still holding its own against the background of a red, white, and blue wallpaper with a design of soldiers.

I love exploring in collage, trying things in a new way, searching to find out how many variations are possible on the same composition element. They're apparently endless. One of the reasons collage is never boring is the constant surprise of discovering a new way of doing something you've done before.

For "Letter to Miss Aiken" (opposite), I used a 19½-inch-square gesso board. Instead of allowing a ribbon of exposed gesso to separate the colors, I cut a band of white paper and let that serve the same function. The result was a very interesting and different textural value from the sort one gets with natural or primed gesso.

When I first tried the red and white gingham table, it looked unsubstantial against the brilliant-colored walls. To give it substance, I tried backing it separately with white paper. I cut a heavy piece to exactly the dimensions of the

Detail of RED, WHITE, AND BLUE

RED, WHITE, AND BLUE

LETTER TO MISS AIKEN

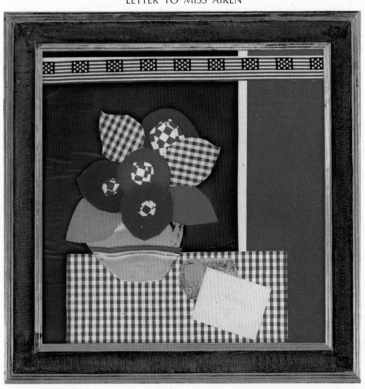

fabric, pasted, and ironed. It worked perfectly. This technique was to be very helpful in the future.

In this strong setting, aluminum foil seemed too thin for the vase, so I used the plastic paper from which I'd cut the mirror in "Think of Me." For the bouquet and leaves, I used brilliant tones that could hold their own against the other colors. I backed the green gingham in the same way I'd backed the tablecloth. It gave the fabric an opaque strength that it did not have in its natural state.

To keep the tray subordinate to the vase, I made it of foil, which I wrinkled so that it would have a still more textured veneer. The green paper marble on the tray brought the greens down into that area of the composition.

At this point in the development of the collage, the eye focused on the center and bottom of the picture. As strong as the background tones were, they were not strong enough to hold their own for a good quarter of the total area.

To draw the eye up to the top of the composition, I used the American flag ribbon. When the ribbon was in a good position, I found that something more was needed on the table. I wanted it to have the geometric precision of the more modern elements but to provide a contrast in feeling. Among the things I'd been saving for future use was a collection of old envelopes, addressed to a Miss Aiken of Worcester, Mass., that I'd discovered in Brandon's Memorabilia, a fascinating shop on the East Side of New York. If you ever happen to be in the city, it's worth a visit. You'll enjoy browsing among the extraordinary collection of decorative cutouts, old valentines, posters, and Victoriana. One of the Miss Aiken envelopes pulled the collage together wonderfully well and gave it its name.

Strangely enough, "Letter to Miss Aiken" successfully accomplished what I'd originally intended to do in "Red, White, and Blue." It was a study in bold colors and precise, hard, unbroken lines.

The frame of "Letter to Miss Aiken" is particularly successful in the way it picks up the blue and silver, and this leads me to a brief digression on the subject of framing. There's a good and economical way of bringing about this merging of collage and frame. It's also fun to do. Just follow the steps shown on pages 42–47.

Remember, when you place elements at the top or sides of a picture, that you must leave space for framing. A quarter of an inch on all sides of your collage will be lost when it is framed. You must always allow for it in the placement of your objects.

Whether you make your own frame or not, always remember that if the frame works for the picture, it will usually work for the room in which it hangs.

Using the Miss Aiken envelope, I began to have an image of what the original Miss Aiken might have been like. A fantasy started to take shape. She had yellow hair, deliciously reminiscent of the Orphan Annie that delighted my childhood. She was ageless in the way that mothers are; friendly in the way the stranger is who starts out by offering you a stick of spearmint on the bus and ends up telling you her life story; witty and amusing (the way your best friend makes *you* feel), and yet mysterious too—the way someone is whom you admire but don't know (Garbo perhaps); and somebody reassuring, like the ump lady down the hall picking up the milk bottles and the newspaper in her panese kimono.

"Miss Aiken" (page 40) is a very big picture: 49½ inches square. The gesso oard was so large that I worked on it on the floor. This is a good way to work. gives a much better perspective when you can look down on your picture nd see it from a distance. Even if you generally work on a table, from time to me put your collage on the floor and look down at it from this new angle.

After setting the backing of small green and large yellow ginghams, I thought might be interesting to translate the compositional elements of a traditional enaissance portrait into modern collage terms. These paintings always include window that looks out over a landscape of the region. I curtained my window ith white edging, gave it a brown gingham ledge, and a pale blue gingham ista.

I wanted a substantial, passive shape for Miss Aiken. I first cut the outline of e head and a large semi-oval for the body out of clay paper. This heavy rawing paper gave the figure a good bulk. You can do the same thing just s effectively with cardboard or any other heavy material; if it isn't naturally hite, it can be primed. The orange gingham for the table could have been acked with paper too, but that would have given it exactly the same density s Miss Aiken. Instead, I doubled the material, which gave it a padded look ather than a rigid weight.

I drew in the simple inked contour lines for Miss Aiken's face and brushed spots of violet paint for eye-coloring. Even if you've never done any sketch-g before, don't be put off by the thought of it. In this sort of picture, the ore fanciful and primitive the drawing, the better. The most difficult step is icking up the pen. Why not try it in easy stages? Keep a pad and, in your spare me or while talking on the phone, start doodling. You will be surprised at ow quickly your inhibitions disappear.

For Miss Aiken's hair, I cut yellow paper in the shape I wanted and pasted it ver the clay paper. The red gingham dress was as shapeless as a sack but ouchingly girlish in a lumpish sort of way. The arms were made with clay aper showing beneath the sleeves. The right one is deliberately narrower an the left to give the illusion that the figure is turned slightly away; this is einforced by having the buttons slant slightly to the right. You don't need to now anything about perspective to make it work. Just move things around ntil they please your eye.

In composing "Miss Aiken" I noticed a few things that might be useful to nybody planning a portrait collage. Placing the figure in the center of the icture gave it a natural dominance, and everything else was planned to keep the center of attention. Large areas were deliberately left free of ornamenta-on. Only small objects were set on the table in the foreground, and Miss iken looms over them.

The elements move around her so that she remains visually as well as physi-lly in the center. The large bouquet on the right, the photograph, and the owerpot on the window ledge form a semicircle that is underscored by a naller circle of decoupage that extends from the lily bottle stopper to the ell to the plum to the strawberry to the pear and plant on the window. Start-g with the red bottle at right and moving all the way to the magenta one at ft, the vivid colors also arc—as do all the flowers from the large one at right

MISS AIKEN

SUNDAY

through the decoupage on the window ledge.

Miss Aiken was a theme I was to return to again and again, each time with a new sense of joy and discovery. This large, doll-like figure has an unending fascination for me. Another collage in which it appears is "Sunday" (opposite).

"Sunday" was done on a gesso of the same large dimensions as the one used in "Miss Aiken"—49½ inches square. I backed it with a combination of red and violet ginghams for the walls; the table was blue gingham. The checks were all the same size: the colors gave them sufficient definition. The picture was to be complex, so I felt it was better not to emphasize their pictorial value by making them different gauges.

I added a window exactly as I had in "Miss Aiken" and cut a rectangle of aluminum foil for the mirror, which I framed in striped ribbon. The mats on the table were a tiny green gingham under a blue gingham with a paper lace mat topping both.

At this early stage, "Sunday" was a study in rectangles. The fabrics were cut in very definite sharp right angles, with no attempt at shredding. Until the figures were established, I did not want to use anything that might compete with them in suppleness.

I cut the two figures in different scales. The one in the mirror was smaller than the one looking into it. This perspective device gives the illusion of distance.

For the real Miss Aiken in the foreground, I cut the yellow paper hair so that one got a rear view of it. The hat was blue paper topped by a decoupage white flower; the dress, an orange gingham of the same gauge as the backing ginghams.

The reflection face and head were treated exactly as they had been in "Miss Aiken." The front view of the hat naturally had a different shape. The decoupage flower on top was also different. The other decoupage decorations were obviously only visible in the mirror. The button and little collar were likewise only visible in reflection, the collar running out of sight under the hair in the rear. Again in compliance with the laws of perspective, the orange gingham dress was cut from a fabric with a smaller check.

Although the structure of the other elements in the picture was like that of the things in "Miss Aiken," there was a compositional difference in the treatment of the decoupage. In this case, it followed the hard lines of the major areas by forming an almost perfect right-angle triangle from the flower on the hat to the plums to the blue flower bottle stopper up to the plant in the window and back to the hat.

Although the ladder-back chair was cut rather freely out of red paper, the shape was selected because it had the same kind of geometric precision that prevailed in the rest of the collage. To complete the composition, I cut a black and white check butterfly, placing it almost in the center of the window.

There is something very reassuring about "Sunday." It has a rounded simplicity of statement that makes me feel that there, within its framework, on that particular day, God's in His heaven and all's right with the world.

MAKING A SIMPLE FRAME

It is marvelously easy to make a frame that will set off any collage perfectly—all you need is a wood frame from a five- and ten-cent store and some of the fabric that you plan to use (or have used) in the collage.

1. All the materials necessary for making the frame.

2. The original frame—an inexpensive item notable only for its straight, squared-off sides.

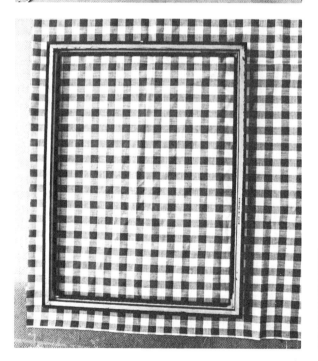

3. Place the frame (glass removed and set aside) face down in a corner of the fabric, leaving a generous margin of cloth.

4. With scissors, cut along one side of the fabric, again leaving a margin of a few inches between it and the frame.

5. Continue cutting around the frame, until you have a piece of fabric slightly larger than the dimensions of the frame.

6. Spread some newspaper on your floor or work table and put the frame face up on it. Spray or brush the frame with glue.

7. Flop the frame over onto the fabric (center it neatly) and press down firmly.

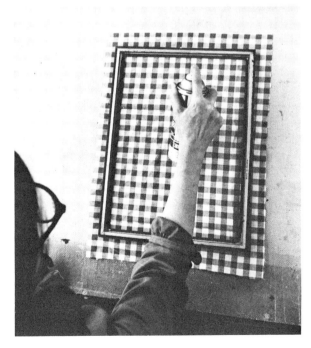

8. When the glue has dried somewhat, spray the back of the frame with glue.

9. Spray the outer and inner edges of the frame. If you are using a spray glue instead of the kind applied with a brush or other applicator, be careful to guide it so that you don't get too much glue on the fabric.

10. Turn one edge of fabric over one side of the frame.

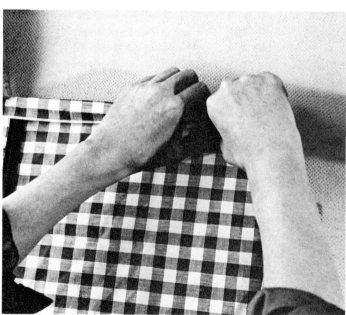

11. Press the fabric firmly down along the outer edge and back of the frame.

12. Continue to the corner.

14. Continue gluing down the fabric in the same manner all around the frame until the fabric is entirely secured to the back of the frame.

3. Make a hospital corner just as if you were making a bed.

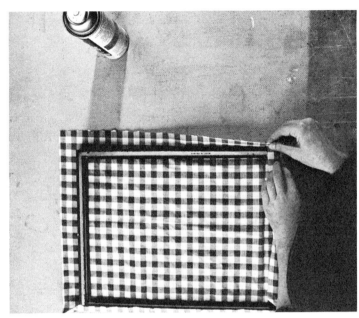

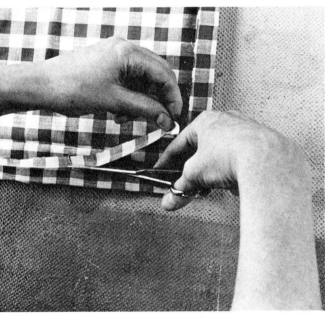

15. When the glue has dried, tidy up by snipping away excess fabric flapping over the edge of the frame.

16. Now start to cut out the fabric inside the frame, again leaving a margin of a few inches. A razor is the best tool for this process.

17. When you have finished cutting out the inside piece, remove it. You can use this in the collage, or save it for another picture.

18. Make a diagonal cut in the fabric in each corner of the frame from the inside edge of the frame to the edge of the fabric.

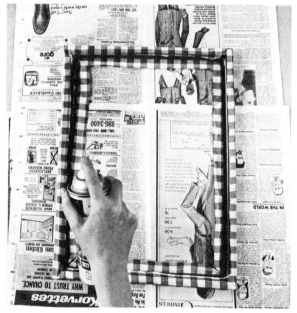

19. With the frame face down, spray the fabric with glue. You don't need to worry if you get too much glue on it, since it won't be visible.

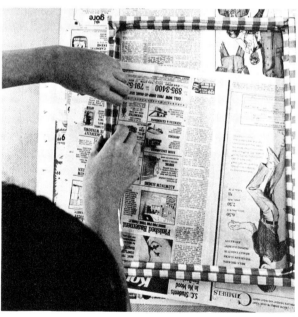

20. Flap the fabric on each side up and over the back of the frame.

1. Press the fabric down securely on the back and
inner edges of the frame and let the glue dry. If necessary,
snip away any excess fabric.

22. The finished frame, upholstered in fabric. When you
are ready, replace the glass in the frame, put the
collage in place, and it's ready to hang.

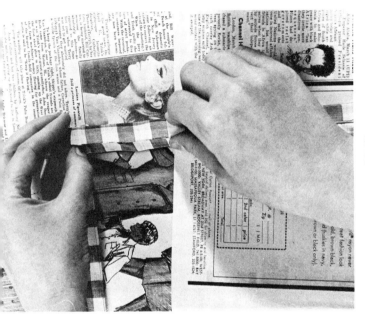

CHAPTER THREE

About the time I began to do collage, my husband and I fell in love with a huge, rambling old wreck of a house, and we've been spending a lot of time since then propping it up, cleaning it out, and getting it aired and heated. Decorating this enchanting old house was a great adventure, and the result of it all is not unrelated to my work in collage.

We had been looking all around the Hamptons on eastern Long Island for a summer place. It had to be big; we have two teen-age boys and two small boys, and we like to have enough room for everybody to get away from everybody else. We looked at a number of houses, but none fitted every need. Either they were too small, or they were too far from the beach for the children, or too far from the church for the staff, or too near the neighbors for me, while my husband kept muttering something about wanting gingerbread architecture and a front porch that Mark Twain would like to sit on.

Then, finally, one day in Southampton, a real estate lady said, "Now I apologize for even showing you this next one. It's in the *most terrible condition,* but you said white elephant, and it's a white elephant if ever there was one." And how right she was. There it stood, an elegant old monster that loomed above the places around it, far too large for the little acre it sat on, its shingled sides denuded of paint by half a century of storms, its driveway no driveway at all, but a ditch with potholes in it. A long gallery ran all along the front and ended

The sitting room in Southampton. From left to right: "Miss Aiken," "Tribute of Love," "Pansies," "The Family." "Reward of Merit," which also hangs in the room, cannot be seen in this view.

an octagonal porch on the sea side—perfect, perhaps, for Mark Twain but, las, sagging and swaying in a sickening way when we set foot on it. The oundation had rotted out from under one end of the house, and there was not a tree on the lot. Inside, because of the uneven floors, all the plaster was cracked and here and there hung in great chunks held up by gray shreds of stained and bilious wallpaper. Naturally, we knew at once we had to have it.

As we picked our way through the dingy rooms, the real estate lady said with some skepticism, "They say that Stanford White designed this place." My husband and I exchanged looks. Of course Stanford White designed it. That's why the rooms flow into each other in such an easy, original way. That accounts for the marvelously balanced staircase. Most of all, it's why it's flooded with light. The house curves in an odd way that you hardly notice. It's only when you start to figure things out that you realize that it follows the path of the sun, so that light streams in all day. The living room was magnificent, with

Our townhouse in New York is full of examples of collage in decorating. Not only do my collages hang on the walls, but some of the rooms have actually become collages themselves.

Above is a detail from the bedroom floor—hundreds of pieces of fabric were pasted down to form a giant patchwork quilt. To do this, the pieces must be cut and fitted together so that they do not overlap, in order to keep the surface flat. Then, many coats of varnish should be applied to protect the surface.

For years we collected beautiful old patchwork quilts simply because we liked them. Then we hit upon the idea of a patchwork room with the quilts covering the walls and ceiling, as well as a patchwork floor. The curtains, shown opposite, were made by taking some of the quilts apart and reassembling them in new patterns.

On pages 52 and 53 are two more views of the bedroom.

a 30-foot ceiling and a circular staircase enclosed in a little tower at one corner of the room. The stairs led up to a balcony that extended across the entire width of the room. Also, there was a bank of stained-glass windows, and the effect, generally, was not unlike that of an early New England Congregational church.

My husband, who rather fancies himself as having some sort of "feeling" for real estate, was ecstatic about the whole thing. "Look," he said gleefully, "the condition that house is in, we'll get it practically free. Remember it's been on the market for years, and nobody nibbled. It's hard to unload a big old barn like that." In his innocence, he failed to reckon with the seller, a shrewd old party who hadn't built his enormous real estate fortune by selling short. Not only did he refuse to come down as much as a dollar; he announced that he wasn't sure he was willing to sell. He did, however, agree to grant us an interview at which we could present our credentials. The time appointed for the pleading of our case was set at nine o'clock of a summer morning; both of us did our best to be enchanting, smiled far more than is normal, and laughed to excess at his pleasantries. My husband, who has no shame, admired at appalling length a certain painting of some cows in a field once he learned that the young lady who was responsible for it was a personal friend of the old gentleman. He even went so far at one point as to say to our host, "Have you noticed that wherever you go in the room, the cows' eyes follow you?" The surprised gentleman had *not* noticed, but was delighted to know it, now it had been called to his attention, and, after we had all walked around the room demonstrating the phenomenon several times, he allowed that our family connections were acceptable and we seemed like the sort of people who would be a credit to the Southampton community so he was willing to let us buy the house at the price originally stated.

Our friends came and looked and usually managed to be polite, but, more often than not, it was clear they were quite horrified by the task we had taken on. It was, however, really a great deal simpler than it seemed. Once we jacked the house up and put a concrete foundation under it, cleared out the fallen plaster, and saw to the heating and wiring, it was all a matter of scraping away the decorative improvements others had put down through the years. In a way we were lucky, of course, that no serious damage had been done. The architecture was original and had escaped the death by modernizing that has so often destroyed good old designs.

Our first decision was to paint the floors and all the woodwork white. For this floor treatment to be successful, you have to apply half a dozen coats of paint, and you must have the time and patience to let it dry and set completely between coats.

In my dressing room, we took another approach—one that was an extension of my work in collage. We covered not only the walls and ceiling but the floor as well with a charming wallpaper in a design of wood violets on green leaves. The wallpaper must be glued down to a smooth floor and coated with seven or eight applications of clear varnish. The effect was so pleasing that we then papered the bedroom floor. Later, in New York, we actually made our bedroom floor into a patchwork quilt, pasting down hundreds of multicolored scraps and patches, and carried the theme throughout the room. Once you start thinking in terms of collage, there's no limit to where your imagination can take you.

n the following pages is a view of our living room. In the foreground is one of two benches we upholstered with silk nd velvet patchwork from a Victorian quilt. The interesting stitchery used to connect the pieces and embroidered on ome is a decorative element in itself, and you could do it yourself.

Below is another view of the living room, showing the second collage-covered bench.

On the opposite page, at top, is a Shirley Temple doll that we consider an engaging example of Pop art of the thirties. She sits in our living room (you can see her in the background on page 55). On the seat of the chair is one of the old patchwork quilts from our collection, and behind the doll is one of several pillows we covered, like the benches, with a collage of fabrics.

Not all collage decorating projects have to be large-scale. The little items shown opposite, below, were easy to make. On the left is a decorative object which I found in a shop full of imaginative things. Bits of various fabrics were cut out and glued to its many surfaces. It was intended to be a doorstop. On the right is an address book covered in patchwork. This was given to me by Luis Perez, who skillfully executed our patchwork-covered room and floor.

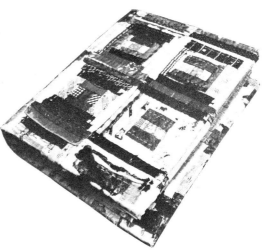

Opposite: The top of this desk was made into a patchwork by rearranging pieces from
another of our quilts. The surface is protected by a slab of glass (which was
removed to make the photograph), so the desk is perfectly functional. Any table top—
end tables, coffee tables, or whatever you like—can be treated in the same way.

Above is another view of the bedroom. Propped up on the suede sofa is an early
nineteenth-century American doll which oddly relates, in my mind's eye, to the figure in
the silvery valentine I used in "Tribute of Love" (page 60). Visible in the corner
is a blanket box, the surface of which has been decorated with decoupage
Edwardian fashion plates and lacquered over, much in the same way as were those
painted and decoupaged cigar boxes fashionable a few decades ago.

THE FAMILY

PANSIES

REWARD OF MERIT

TRIBUTE OF LOVE

Our sitting room in the Southhampton house (page 49) is another example of how a room can grow out of collage and collage, out of a room. In this case it would be impossible to say which came first, for both were forming in my mind at the same time and I used the same fabrics for each. An advantage in knowing where pictures are going is that you can introduce into the pictures themselves fabrics from the walls and furnishings of the room for which they are intended. Because "Miss Aiken" was sunny, friendly, and cozy, she seemed to belong in the sitting room. Four other collages were to find their place in the sitting room: "The Family," "Pansies," "Reward of Merit," and "Tribute of Love."

The direct inspiration for "The Family" (opposite) was an old photograph of sisters. They were the sort of people who might once have lived in a house like ours. I loved the old-fashioned feeling of the picture, and was particularly enchanted by the wavy laciness of the girls' hair and dress.

I selected a gesso board measuring 23½ by 35½ inches—the right proportions for the space over the fireplace. The backing was predominantly the same lavender and white checked gingham I'd used for the buttons on Miss Aiken's dress (and for the sitting room walls). The remainder of the backing was a blue and white checked gingham. For the table, I backed a turquoise gingham with white clay paper to give it a nontransparent weight. All three ginghams had checks of the same gauge. I didn't back any of the fabrics in "The Family" except for the turquoise gingham. I use the technique only when it's absolutely necessary, because it makes the materials too rigid, almost unnatural. They can lose the quality that first attracted me to them. For example, in this work, the unbacked green and white gingham leaves in the elaborate bouquet give an illusion of transparency.

As usual, most of the materials and objects I intended to use were already collected in my studio, and the work went fast. Before deciding on its final location in the picture, I tried the photograph of the girls in various relationships to the other elements. The second photograph was an old tintype of a couple and in my imagination they became the girls' parents. When you work with photographs, it's important not to place them too quickly and arbitrarily. Keep shifting and testing until you find the right balance.

The photographs were very heavily mounted. To soften the stiffness of the girls' picture, I used aluminum foil matting. At the same time, I changed the shape from an oblong to an oval. I cut the center out of an oval white paper lace mat and used the border over the foil. It not only cut the reflection of the metallic paper but was also an improvised impression of a period frame.

I framed the couple in a very heavy silver paper frame. If you can't find this kind of frame (mine came from Brandon's Memorabilia in New York; they specialize in this sort of paper product), you can attain the same effect by doing exactly what I did with the girls but substituting a silver paper lace mat for the white one.

Most of the other objects were used more for their abstract decorative qualities than for any literal resemblance to reality. That even applied to the Victorian playing cards. The decoupage speckled egg and conch shell provided the link between abstraction and the very real photographs: they were realistic, yet almost abstract in color and shape.

As complicated as "The Family" may look, it was actually very easy to execute. The composition emerged, as do all others, from the scrambling of elements. In scrambling, be generous. It's wiser to start with too much than with too little. In this collage, I tried many more things than those you see in the finished work. If pasting is the last thing done, then things can be eliminated and saved for another picture. The wonderful thing about using objects you really love is that they're never wasted. If they don't fit into one collage, they will into a future one.

Ever since my first use of decoupage, I have loved the special quality it lends to everything in which it appears. I'd always wanted to use it as the dominant element in a collage, and the wish was finally realized when I happened upon some prints of clustered pansies.

For "Pansies" (page 60), I used a 20- by 24-inch gesso board. I primed the board with white acrylic paint, so those areas that might be exposed would have a lacquered sheen.

At the beginning, the decoupage was the only thing I was completely certain I would use. The pansies were so bold that it seemed a good idea to have some general principles in mind before taking the next step. I would have to be careful not to use elements that would either overwhelm or be overwhelmed by them. Because of their brilliant color, the other colors would have to be muted but still capable of holding their own in any large buildup of detail.

After backing the gesso with lavender paper and some of the lavender gingham that was on the sitting room walls (leaving a ribbon of the primed white between the two), I was ready for the decoupage. The pansies were especially intricate. I decided to use two of the clusters to get more fullness in the blossoms and variety in the color. The first thing I did was cut around the outside edges of flowers and leaves. The interior was a lacy network of stem and leaf. I could not use my scissors on it without the risk of cutting into the delicate greenery. The best instrument for this is a tool called a Stanley 199 A Retractable Razor, which has a razor blade fitting into a handle and can be found in any hardware store.

For the table, I selected a fabric with a delicate rose print that could hold its own and still not compete with the pansies.

The vase presented a bit of a problem. A solid color might dominate the bouquet; silver might distract from it. I felt the proper balance could only be achieved by the feeling of Victorian pattern. I recalled saving some old wallpaper with a very delicate print. I dug it out and examined it; it had exactly the right quality. Another piece of old wallpaper became a mat under the vase. I inserted a white paper mat between the two prints. Then I mounted an old valentine on yellow gift paper and set it alongside the vase on the mat.

I enjoyed what was happening in the collage. There was a lovely melange of old and new, of realism and fantasy. In this medium, you can do things with color and texture that you could never achieve in painting.

Arranging the flowers in an old-fashioned nosegay seemed like a delicious idea. I cut the border frill away from a circular paper lace mat and placed the pansies in it. I scattered circles of colored paper among the lace and backed the arrangement with a shredded mat of gingham. Its violet checks were the same color as the backing paper. Decoupage butterflies accented by magenta dots were spaced about the background, and the picture was finished with a

Detail of PANSIES

red and yellow flower cut from a linen print and placed onto the pink mat on the table.

Of all my flower collages, this is my favorite. It has innocence and strength, and reaches outward like sunlight.

My object in "Reward of Merit" (page 60) was to construct a still life mainly of fabrics with flower prints. I used a 24-inch-square board and backed it with a combination of large and small checked orange and white gingham. For the table, I used a violet gingham of the same gauge as the smaller orange. On one side of the picture, I laid a border of white eyelet with a thin ribbon embroidered in purple over it.

The vase was cut from the same paper as the mat in "Pansies" and formed another decorative link between the two collages. Because the blue flower print mat was strong enough to hold its own against the gingham table, there was no need for a place mat.

For the bouquet, I shredded a jagged circle of a fabric printed with brightly colored flowers against a dark background. I reversed the order of the elements in "Pansies" and set the frill on top of instead of behind the flowers. From a linen print, I cut individual white and pink flowers, leaving a little of the black field around each.

Once this was done, I gathered together all of the other elements. The decoupage butterflies came from an old print. The figurines are shell dolls cut out of a postcard I found at the Museum of the City of New York and quite similar to two that I own. The comb is magenta paper, the patterned perfume bottle is old wallpaper. The decoupage flower stopper reminds me to mention that seed catalogs are a marvelous source of pictures to be used in this fashion.

The flower on the table is another reference to "Pansies." It is made of the same fabric as the one in that picture but, in this case, I didn't cut away all of the black background. It had to relate to the backgrounds of the flowers in the bouquet.

The *Reward of Merit* certificate is the sort that used to be given to school children. I found it one day while browsing in the Argosy Bookshop in New York. I've never been quite sure of what the other artifact was. The writing, though very much obscured, is clearly German. It might once have served as the top of a cardcase.

Detail of REWARD OF MERIT

The last picture in the gingham room is "Tribute of Love" (page 60). Although this picture combines many of the fabrics used in the other collages in the gingham room, it has a quality uniquely its own. This stems mainly from the elaborate silvery valentine inscribed *Tribute of Love,* from which the title of the collage came. This sparkling extravaganza of lace surrounds a fantasy child from long ago, bundled up in snowy ermine and, surely, forever shielded from time and all the harsh realities of growing up.

The gesso board, measuring 20 by 24 inches, was backed with turquoise and white checked gingham and turquoise linen. The gingham is the gingham of the table in "The Family." The spatial relationships of the two backing materials, the ribbons of gesso, and the table areas are almost identical in "Pansies," "Reward of Merit," "Tribute of Love," and even "The Family"— though the last is a horizontal picture and the others are vertical.

Detail of TRIBUTE OF LOVE

The flowerpot in "Tribute of Love" was cut from the fabric that is the bouquet in "Reward of Merit." The mat in the former was the center of the frill in the latter, and the flower on it relates to the bouquet in "Tribute of Love," as the same fabric was used for both. The calico background for the plant is the fabric used for the bouquet in a picture I've already discussed (which does not hang in the gingham room), "Constancy" (page 32).

For the decoupage flowers, I wanted the same three-dimensional quality as in "Pansies," but the pale colors of these flowers did not stand out with a comparable vibrancy. I pasted down the two hyacinths but decided to paste down the violets only on the bottom of the decoupage, leaving the top (or lower) free of glue so that it could stand away from the surface of the collage. The decoupage shells and butterflies completed the composition. In doing this type of lightly pasted collage in which your objects are not firmly glued down, it can be most effective to frame them with the glass raised slightly off the picture. It gives another dimensional effect. In fact, all collages benefit by this kind of framing. It not only permits textures to breathe, but, for some mysterious reason, it gives colors a truer brilliancy.

When the sitting room was finished with the lavender and white check gingham echoed in the various pictures, the effect was unusual and personal. It's the kind of room that invites one to linger.

The most successful rooms in a house are those that you naturally gravitate to because you feel coziest in them. This is how we feel about the gingham room. We also find ourselves adding things to it. Photographs of family and friends, as well as things we discover on antiquing expeditions. The walls are lined with our favorite books, many of which belonged to me as a child, and which now are enjoyed by our children. The overall feeling of the room itself is a kind of collage that is lived in and enjoyed.

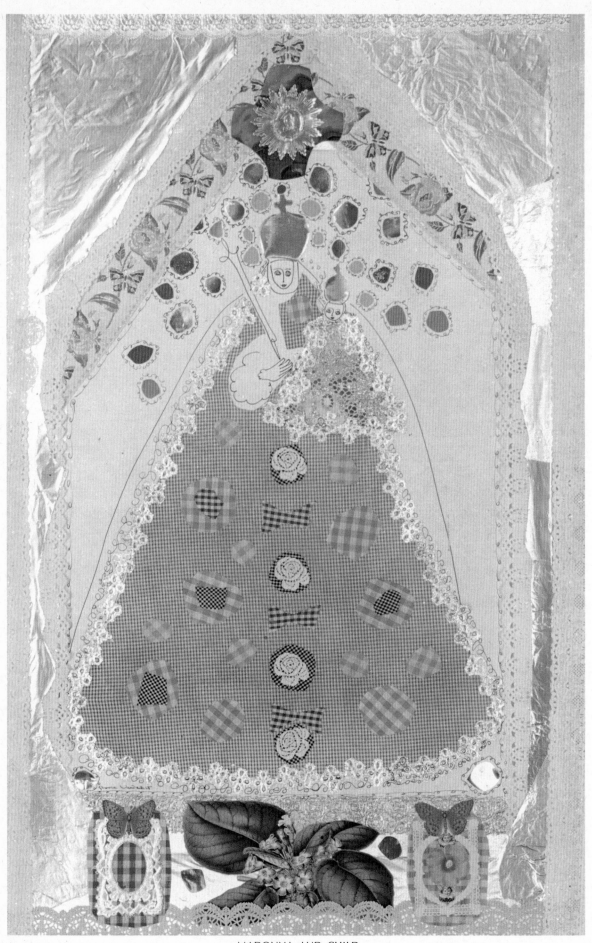

MADONNA AND CHILD

CHAPTER FOUR

The theme of the Madonna and Child has always been a great source of inspiration for artists. Medieval and Renaissance painters and sculptors have left us an astonishing heritage of work on this subject, and each succeeding age has dealt with the subject in its own distinctive manner. Apart from their value as religious illustration and actual function as objects of veneration, these works embody a universal theme of motherhood. In my own painting, I'd often been drawn to the subject. It was inevitable that one day I would want to do a Madonna in collage (opposite).

I drew the mother and child on clay paper, freely sketching the faces, hand, and scepter. I wanted to capture the primitive quality of pre-Giotto painting. It was a period when directness of feeling, sculptural qualities, and costume textures took precedence over realism in representation. Gold leaf and jewels were applied liberally to the surfaces of the pictures. It is a style that lends itself to reinterpretation in collage.

I hope I've persuaded you to try your hand at drawing. If not, there are alternatives. You might find a picture of a mother and child and cut out the heads to use in your picture. With slightly more daring, you might trace them. When you've found the faces you want in a photograph or painting, place a sheet of tracing paper over them and trace only the bolder outlines of the features—lips, nose, eyes, chin, shape of head. These simple contour lines should be made with a hard pencil. Then, with a soft pencil, blacken the back of your paper everywhere that the drawing appears. Place the sheet, blackened side down, on the material to which you want to transfer the drawing. Carefully go over your drawing with a fine, hard point. Lift away the tracing paper, and the transfer will have been completed. The last step is to go over the drawing in India ink to highlight the lines.

Detail of MADONNA AND CHILD

After I did the drawing for "Madonna and Child," I cut out clay paper in the shape of a Gothic arch, which I then pasted on a gesso measuring 40 by 20 inches. I used the clay paper instead of doing it directly on the backing board not only to give the arch an added dimension, but also because clay paper takes ink so well.

For the Madonna's dress I cut two pieces of a green and white gingham. The larger panel was for the bulk of the skirt from the child down; the smaller ne was for the shoulder above the child. I decorated the skirt with circles of gingham in a variety of colors and gauges. Almost like fasteners down the center of the skirt, I alternated brown gingham bows with black gingham circles. In the center of each circle I set a small rose cut from the pattern of a piece of white paper lace.

For the child's gown, I pasted a length of silver lace that I'd found at a remnant sale over aluminum foil. I outlined both gowns with edging cut from silver paper lace mats. The crowns were silver plastic paper topped with bright red wrapping paper jewels. The jewels beneath the canopy were cut from the plastic paper and colored mat composition paper.

The canopy itself was made of a richly embroidered ribbon. Overlapping this and running the length of the figure, I used white paper lace backed with the plastic paper.

The plastic paper medallion was topped by a gold paper sunburst (found in a greeting card shop) with a candy coin wrapper in its center. The different intensities of each metallic paper created a richly shimmering contrast of textures.

In the telling, this encrustation of layer upon layer of material seems more complicated than it was in the making. Keep in mind that you are the sole arbiter of how far to go. You can stop at any point that looks right to you.

In this collage the backing came after much of the detail. I pasted sheets of aluminum foil from the edge of the clay paper to the edge of the gesso and constructed a platform for the Madonna with a strip of gold paper lace. I curtained the entire picture with silver paper lace.

A large decoupage primrose was placed at the Madonna's feet. I added lavender paper circles and ran a border of blue paper lace along the very bottom of the picture. I set two ovals—one of red and one of pink gingham—on either side of the primrose and placed over them two frames of paper lace. To add color, I put a decoupage butterfly on top of each of them.

The vivid red gingham held its own in the empty frame, but the gentler pink faded away. The visual disparity made the collage seem a little off-balance. To set it right, I added a decoupage violet flower to the center of the pink-backed frame, and decided the collage was finished.

This is an example of stopping work on a picture long before all possibilities had been explored. I could have continued and developed it into an elaborate layer-on-layer encrustation of shapes and colors. But I stopped at this early stage because I wanted the picture to be a simple statement combining the primitive and austere with the textural reality of fabric and lace.

One day, I chanced upon a marvelous piece of iconography at Schatzki's, a shop that deals in old and rare manuscripts and books. It was the figure of a saint in a bishop's miter holding a heart in his hand. Dating from the fifteenth century, it was both embroidered and painted. The face and the word "Veritas" were painted, the rest done in needlepoint.

The delicate petit point frame of passion flowers somehow reminded me of Christmas. It's a double holiday for my husband and me, because it's also our wedding anniversary. Knowing his liking for icons, I thought this saint would make a perfect present for him. At the time, I was working on collage Madonnas. What a splendid combination the two would make. Certainly, the Madonna and Child represent what the Christmas season is all about.

Detail of CHRISTMAS PRESENT

"Christmas Present" (opposite) ended up being an extravagant adventure in collage. I used an enormous stretched canvas of about 40 by 60 inches—it had to be large to hold all the mementos I planned to put on it. As I've said, anything firm enough to hold your objects can serve as a backing.

In this case, I used two layers of clay paper. First, I cut a large piece in the shape of an arch and placed it on the canvas. I then drew the Madonna and Child on another piece and cut it out in silhouette. I mounted this on mirror paper, creating an exposed border, like an iridescent shadow, all around the drawing. The construction was positioned on the original clay paper.

Beneath the figures, the clay paper was covered with gold gift wrapping paper to create a pedestal. I placed the saint beneath this and, in the center of the gold paper, I cut an area large enough to show as much of the embroidery as I felt necessary. It changed the original rectangular shape into an oval that framed the passion flowers.

I still hadn't settled on what other elements I wanted to use. I never really did. The collage just grew and grew until it looked finished.

I covered the entire canvas right up to the edge of the larger clay paper with many layers of crumpled aluminum foil: this gave an overall sparkling silver and gold Christmas look. I mounted red paper on one half of the skirt and pink on the other, and the colors showed through an overlaid filigree of silver paper lace. Once I'd started, one layer led to another. White paper lace embroidered the silver lace; tiny gold paper bows and red and lavender paper Christmas balls ornamented the skirt. A fantasy of color and fabric and paper materials of every description emerged; more than anything else, it resembled the bursts of color and elaborate details of a Mexican shrine.

The infant's dress was green paper backed with clay paper for bulk, with gold paper lace spread over it. I embroidered further with lavender paper bows pinned by turquoise paper circles, and scattered paper bows and balls over the skirt. Ivory paper flowers, cut from an old valentine, completed the infant.

The sprig of flowers held by the virgin was made of multicolored papers cut in discs and leaves. Her crown was made of gold paper mounted on red paper resting in turn on green plastic paper. The child's crown was mounted on pink paper and red plastic paper. At the foot of the figures, I put a shelf of gold paper lace encrusted with gold medallions backed with colored paper. Over golden pendants, I unrolled a ribbon of yellow paper lace emblazoned with gold filigree. Rich gold paper medallions backed by bright colors were suspended from the yellow ribbon.

The saint was in the center of the panel beneath that. I mounted an old sampler cross on green paper and put it beside the embroidery. I framed an old German engagement card in gold paper and placed it on the other side. At the bottom of the pedestal I mounted pieces of gold lace on silver plastic paper and linked them by a chain of gold snowflakes on pink paper. Over this I put decoupage and freely cut shapes of blossoms cut from colored composition paper.

To make the curtains, layers of paper lace and ribbons were built up with colored paper and decoupage and medallions and sentimental and religious cards.

Because this was a very personal greeting to my husband, I added elements meaningful to us. The photograph of the children and me was framed in the

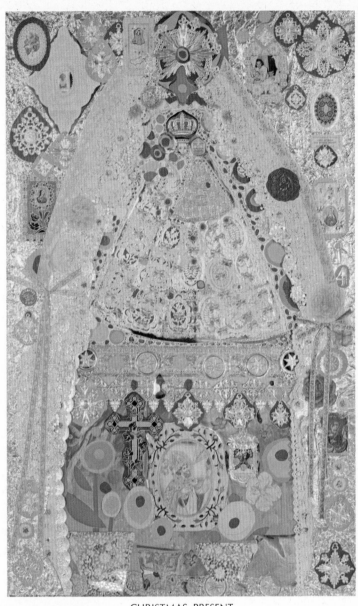

CHRISTMAS PRESENT

HAPPY BIRTHDAY
A birthday present for Mrs. Samuel P. Peabody.

same flowers I'd used on the Christ Child's dress. A childhood photograph of me was used to balance that picture. Because it was a fading black and white and the more recent one was a color snapshot, I framed it more ornamentally. It was placed on a ribbon and mounted on plastic mirror paper. The entire thing was enclosed in pink and white paper filigree.

The St. Constanzia religious card had a symbolic meaning in terms of our marriage. The golden 4 was the number of the years we had been married, the Bronx Zoo tag was a souvenir from an outing with Carter and Anderson, and the bus ticket to San Simeon was from a trip we had made with our big sons Stan and Chris, several years before.

As I proceeded, it became apparent that I'd been reaching for the very special ornateness of a jeweled, golden icon. The collage had taken on a life of its own and a form that could not easily be duplicated or precisely described. I followed my intuition, allowing it to lead me toward an indefinable objective that was at once aesthetic and extremely personal.

To do work as complex as this, a collection from which you can select is a necessity. The work itself is so demanding that if you were forced to search for objects to use, the momentum would be lost, and the collage might not be completed.

From a distance, "Christmas Present" has the shimmering appearance of molten gold, somewhat like a high altar in an especially rich cathedral. It's when one moves close that the details become apparent. One becomes aware of the beauty of the mementos and the charm of the intimate and personal effects. Wyatt says that in case of fire, it's this possession he would run for first.

"Happy Birthday" (page 71) is another such work of love. Somewhere I happened upon a small lacy card with the monogram J. P. embroidered in beads. It made me think immediately of my friend, Mrs. Samuel P. Peabody, whose first name is Judy. What a pleasure it would be to build a collage around it as a birthday present for her.

Although it was early autumn and her birthday wasn't until May, I started collecting things. From Sam, her husband, I got a black and white photograph of Judy as a child and a color shot of him with their daughter, Elizabeth. At Anne Benjamin's Antique Shop on Third Avenue, I found a little Victorian shadow box with the words, "out of friendship" and a needlepoint picture of a rose and the word "love." The "happy birthday" handkerchief came from a department store, the lace doily from my mother's collection. With these elements assembled, I was ready to start work.

I didn't paste anything down until I was absolutely certain it was what I wanted and where I wanted it to be. That included the background colors. On a gesso measuring about 25 by 36 inches, I tried many colors, including a red, before deciding on the yellow and green ginghams. The colors of spring flowers, like yellow daffodils, reminded me of Judy.

The lavender gingham dressing table posed two small problems. In scrambling the elements, I discovered that the original size was too small to hold everything that had to go on it. I extended it by cutting two small strips of gingham and adding them to the ends of the first piece. Also, the material was too flimsy. The shadows of the other fabrics beneath it showed. With so many ob-

Detail of HAPPY BIRTHDAY

jects to be set against it, this created an unnecessary clutter. Backing the gingham with clay paper gave it the necessary density.

I cut the picture of Sam and Elizabeth into the shape of an oval and mounted it on some flowered wallpaper left over from the redecoration of a little powder room in Southampton. A silver and white paper lace frame was set over this. The needlepoint rose was framed in paper reinforced red gingham. I cut Sam's signature from a letter and placed it at the top of the frame, along with a heart from the same ribbon I used in "Red, White, and Blue" (page 37).

Most of the rest of the collage was done in the usual way. Before deciding on the blossoming flowers, I did try many fabrics and pieces of decoupage. The ones I finally settled on had very much the sort of delicacy I've always associated with Judy.

When I'd finished placing everything that I thought I wanted to use, I discovered a need for something more. I didn't want it to merely be another decorative addition. It had to be something relevant.

Some time before, a photograph of Judy appeared in the newspaper. I liked it so much that I'd had it framed. It was the perfect thing for "Happy Birthday," but it was newsprint. From my childhood, I recalled pasting things from the newspapers in an album. The glue often left a stain. I hated the thought that the picture might be ruined. I had to take the chance. Nothing else would work as well.

I assembled the background without gluing—an oval of black gingham, a larger oval of paper lace, several layers of mirror paper, and the photograph backed with aluminum foil and framed in silver and white paper lace. I pasted layer upon layer until arriving at the picture. I took the can of glue and sprayed it from a distance, so that the clipping was covered with a thin, fine coat. The result exceeded my hopes. Not only was there no stain, but this gingerly approach actually gave a delightful, raised, three-dimensional feeling to the newsprint.

There were so many elements in "Happy Birthday" that an enormous amount of scrambling was necessary before I settled on what seemed to be the best composition. It was such a delicate one that it made the actual pasting rather difficult. If one of the elements was moved even a fraction of an inch when replaced after applying the glue, the whole picture might be ruined. One must look at this sort of collage for a long time—take a mental picture—before starting to paste. If you have a Polaroid camera, it is a good idea to take an actual snapshot.

The shadow box was one of the last things left to be glued. It was so heavy that it simply wouldn't hold to the backing. I finally decided to put a picture hook into the gesso and hang it on that. I again applied paste, piled several heavy books on it, and let it set overnight. This ingenious approach worked perfectly, and at last report "out of friendship" was still adhering very nicely.

Collage for the Bennett Cerfs.
Mrs. Cerf asked me to make a collage using letters and other treasured mementos of the Cerfs' friend Moss Hart. I built the work around a large red heart that had greeted the Cerfs when they arrived at Round Hill, Jamaica, to visit the Harts. The happy spirit of the time was captured in the photograph by Richard Avedon.

There is a special delight in making this sort of personal present for friends, for they are touched to receive something that obviously demands such individual thought, care, and planning. For the Joshua Logans (opposite) I kept in mind that their apartment is in reds, greens, and magentas, with a Victorian feeling.

Detail of TO NEDDA AND JOSH

TO NEDDA AND JOSH
Present for the Joshua Logans.

Collages make marvelously personal, individual presents. I did the one pictured opposite for my godchild, Elizabeth Peabody, for Christmas. It is composed of wallpapers, paper lace, and Victoriana—and all the elements are paper.

Above are some enlarged details: the cherubs topping the letters of *Elizabeth;* the little doll figure from a turn-of-the-century advertisement for Prescott pianos; a bit of the rich floral applique around the word *love;* and the whimsical little Christmas card adorned with a glittering paper four-leaf clover. The background is a page from an old oriental manuscript.

SOUVENIR
Present for Mr. and Mrs. Arthur Hornblow.

Present for Mrs. Charles Birdsong.

Present for Mrs. Dominick Dunne.

Present for the Charles Chaplins.

CHAPTER FIVE

There is probably no era of history in which the adornment of self reached greater heights than during the reign of Queen Elizabeth I of England. It was inevitable, once I started making elaborately ornamented figures, that I would find the subject of Elizabethan court ladies and gentlemen exciting. Portraits of the period show us costumes that are themselves fantasies of lace, embroidery, brocades, passementerie, gold, and jewels, and these suited me perfectly.

For my first Elizabeth (opposite) I used a gesso measuring 60 by 40 inches and primed it because I planned large areas of exposed gesso. I sketched the figure directly on the gesso. I wanted to cut clay paper in the shape of the clothes and use it as backing for the fabrics. (I use clay paper because it is good to draw on, but any paper will serve.) In addition to adding sturdiness, the paper-backed pieces would be easier to paste and iron on.

Around Elizabeth's head was a circle of lavender and white gingham. After the paste dried, I cut it in points so that starlike rays would radiate from the head. When I tried it, it was too small proportionally for the figure. I put it aside and cut a much larger circle of blue and white gingham.

The crown was aluminum foil, the jewels colored gift paper mounted on clay paper. I left margins to draw filigree in India ink on the clay paper and around the colored paper. The purpose was to suggest the glitter of gems.

I placed the blue halo around the head and the crown on it. The smaller circle of lavender points I used as a ruff around the neck. It amused me to build up a regal Elizabethan costume in a fabric as humble as gingham. I called the collage "Lady in Gingham."

I cut two large clay paper panels for the sleeves, two for the skirt, and a fourth for the underskirt. I mounted the halo blue gingham on the sleeves and a large gauge of the ruff shade of lavender on the skirt. For the moment, I did nothing with the underskirt.

For the floor, I wanted to simulate the checkerboard marble that is so characteristic of Tudor palaces. I cut a strip of black and white gingham and laid it across the bottom of the gesso. It was too light to give the illusion of heavy marble. I found a much sturdier black and white fabric in which the checks were the same size as those in the gingham. Instead of simply overlaying it, I cut it into squares and placed them on top of the gingham, allowing it to show around them. The squares were deliberately cut in odd sizes to give a feeling of age. Even in the most palatial residences, the passage of time brings repairs that mar the geometric precision of the floor. The doorway was created by framing the rest of the gesso in blue gingham; the woodwork was white paper lace outlined with silver paper lace.

For the embroidery of the costume I wanted sumptuousness stated in terms of paper and gingham. The halo was encrusted with white paper lace points and encircled by silver blossoms. The neck was collared in silver paper lace, which also fanned out over the top of the lavender ruff. Small points of white paper lace encroached on the edge of the ruff. The gingham sleeves were covered with an overlay of spidery white paper lace and appliquéd with silver flowers. The clay paper hands were pasted lightly to make them stand away from the figure. The cascading jewels and rings were treated exactly like the crown jewels. The terminating medallion balanced the coronet. It was made of backed aluminum foil, pink gingham, plastic mirror paper, and a gem of matted purple paper.

The bodice details were applied directly to the gesso without clay paper. The multihued gift paper ribbons and bows were surrounded by silver paper flowers highlighted in India ink.

The skirt was encrusted with circle and leaf shapes cut from both its own lavender gingham and that of the ruff. The glow of the underskirt emanated from paper lace backed with aluminum foil. It was finished off with a double row of blue paper ribbons at the hem. The skirt and sleeves were outlined in silver lace.

When it was finished, the dress was so alive that it made the bare gesso look dull. In order to decorate the space without completely covering the white areas, I used some paper lace mats that had butterfly shapes as part of their pattern. I cut the bodies away and backed them with gingham and aluminum foil. The flowers were gingham discs mounted on foil, with the bold black check of the floor brought up in their centers.

"Lady in Gingham" is actually an impression of a dress of the period. Made of anachronistic materials, it still succeeds in looking Elizabethan.

For "The Necklace" (page 87), I again drew the figure directly on a large 60- by 40-inch gesso. Instead of priming in white, I painted undercoats of key colors— yellow for the background, red for the skirt, violet for the sleeves, rose for the bodice, pale lavender for the headdress.

The ruff was covered with gold paper lace. Because the lace does not come in pieces that large, it had to be applied in sections. It was appliquéd with

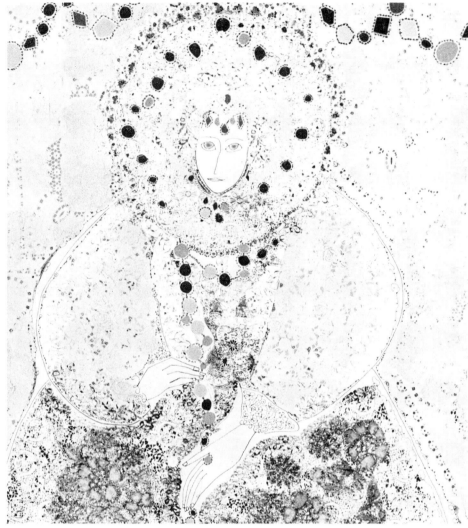

Detail of THE NECKLACE

silver paper lace, and a halo of silver lace went around it from shoulder to shoulder.

The lavender paint of the headdress showed through the filigree of three different kinds of paper lace: silver, gold, and white. The jewels, hanging pendant-like over the brow, were colored paper pasted directly on the gesso. The other ruff and headdress jewels were backed with clay paper and surrounded by swirls of India ink.

I used white paper lace to cover the violet sleeves completely. From another piece of white lace with a rose pattern, I cut the flowers and scattered them over the first layer of lace. To give them a richness, the sleeves are outlined in silver paper lace. They achieved the look and texture of rich fabric without using any cloth.

For half the bodice I used a heavily embossed gold paper filigreed with silver lace; for the other half I set a very heavy application of silver lace directly on the coat of rose paint. I was careful to leave an area of exposed gesso, where the jewels of the necklace would eventually be placed.

Before approaching the skirt, I drew in the hands and cuff, leaving a border of unadorned gesso around them. This was also my intention with the necklace. It seemed to me that in a work this ornate, highlights could be achieved by utter simplicity.

I had not yet done any gluing and would do none until the very end. I constantly experimented with the balance of decor, interchanging textures and patterns. I removed and replaced until the very moment before applying the glue.

The skirt was the major challenge. Pieces of delicate silvery-gold paper lace covered the entire red underpainting. This in turn was appliquéd with panels of a bright, heavy gold lace. A third gold pattern hemmed the skirt and outlined the blank areas around hand, sleeve, and space reserved for the necklace.

The result was rich but still not rich enough. From a length of silver and white lace fabric, I cut the flowers and leaves, so closely that almost none of the linking net remained. Used as embroidery, it gave exactly the right degree of textural enrichment to the dress.

All of the jewels of the necklace were cut from colored paper and pasted directly on the gesso. Only the ring was mounted on clay paper, because I wanted it to have a distinctly different feeling. I tried out many medallions before deciding on the one I ultimately used. It had a base of aluminum foil under a clay paper star with the points terminating in colored paper jewels. On the star there was another disc of foil surmounted by a candy wrapper and red gift paper.

The floor was again foil. The yellow walls were coated with pieces of white paper lace. The looping chain of jewels was made of colored paper mounted on clay paper.

Not until everything was set did I apply the finishing touches in paint and ink. With ink I drew in the bows on the bodice and the highlighting swirls around the necklace jewels. So that the ruff would stand away from the yellow and lace background, I used orange acrylic and painted dots inside the spaces in the silver lace halo.

When "The Necklace" was finished, I thought I'd said all I wanted to say about Elizabeth. But I was wrong. I continued to explore the collage possibilities of that decorative, elegant age.

I've always thought of "Elizabeth the Queen" (opposite) and "Cavalier" (page 89) as a pair. The actual creative procedure for both was not very different from the method used on the other Elizabethan pictures.

The figures were drawn directly on gesso boards of roughly the same dimensions as those used for the "Lady in Gingham" and "The Necklace." However, they did differ from their predecessors—and they presented very special problems that I enjoyed working out.

"Elizabeth" was actually inspired by an old remnant of lace fabric big enough to do the skirt for a large figure in one piece. I painted the skirt area in lavender and cut the fabric to its size. I appliquéd it with red and green paper bows and circles. The other bows were made by crossing small bits of lavender and blue ribbons and fastening a silver flower to them.

I decided on an aluminum foil floor and cut it out so that it ran to the very edge of the skirt. I painted the sleeves pale blue, and, in order to make the skirt stand forward, I decided to have a cape of the same blue run the length of the figure on each side. I used the blue paint on gesso until I reached the area where the silver foil started. Foil, of course, would not take paint in the same way, so I cut composition paper approximately the same shade of blue and

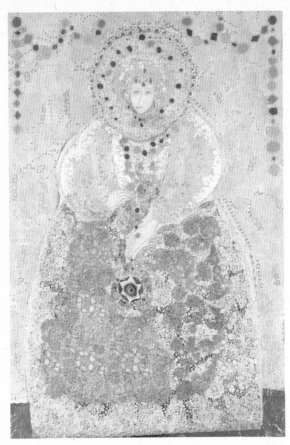

THE NECKLACE

ELIZABETH THE QUEEN

THE HEADDRESS

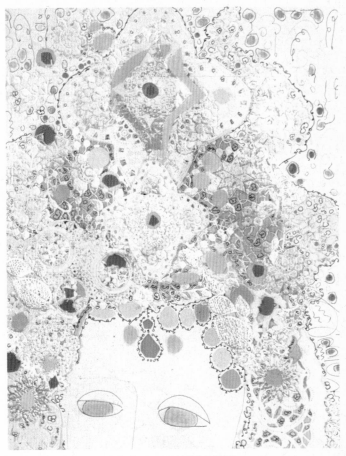

Detail of THE HEADDRESS

Detail of CAVALIER

glued it over the foil. I then applied gold paper lace to the entire cape and sleeve area.

I wanted this collage to have a pale blue and silver feeling in contrast to the heavy yellow gold of "The Necklace." I imposed only the most delicate laces sparingly so that it was light and airy rather than heavy with encrustation. I lightly penned in several tiers of swirls and circles and then dotted red and blue and pink paint over them. It created a delicate glow that was extended the length of the entire figure by a fringe of spidery silver lace that was also speckled with spots of blue and red paint.

The thing I enjoyed most about "Cavalier" was executing all of the architectural details using only the materials of collage without any sketching or painting. I drew *in* paper instead of *on* paper.

I cut panels of raspberry paper to represent the top surfaces of the steps. For the sides, I striped pink with magenta.

The wainscoting was aluminum foil bordered by blue and magenta paper. To give the walls texture and definition, I used alternately the front and rear sides of the foil.

Doing the stockings was very satisfying. After I drew the figure, I contemplated covering the legs in a patterned fabric or paper cut to their shapes. But it occurred to me that it would be more visually exciting to create my own pattern. Although the result looks formidable, the work was actually very easy.

I cut out many clay paper diamonds in different sizes and I covered them with smaller diamonds of colored clay paper, leaving enough margin to do India ink curlicues around each of them. Using the small dark red pieces along the sides gave the legs the illusion of rounded shape. The garters were crescents of red terminating in crimson balls. The result was both decorative and droll.

I mounted and ironed the hat and shoes before placing them on the gesso. As I've said, ironing on these large pictures is rather cumbersome. It's best to back the pieces with clay paper (or any other heavy paper) before pasting them into the collage.

At the very start I drew the face and with an orange crayon colored the beard, hair, and brows. As the costume grew more brilliant, the face diminished. Sandwiched between hat and ruff, the features tended to disappear. To bring them back into focus, I cut pieces of orange paper to highlight the hair. With the addition of this simple collage element, the face was able to hold its own graphically.

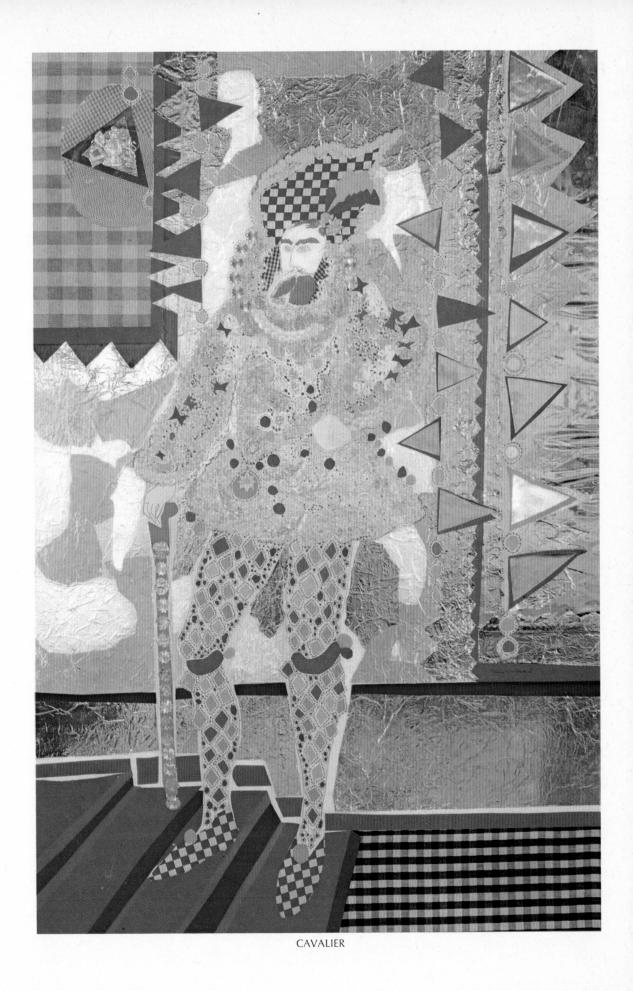

CAVALIER

Detail of COURT DWARF, SEATED

Detail of COURT DWARF, SEATED

"Court Dwarf, Seated" (page 92) was done on a gesso measuring 27½ by 21½ inches. It's a work that has more drawing than most of those included in this book. It achieves a balance between elements of drawing and of collage.

I started by drawing the figure in pen and ink. From paper lace place mats, I cut sections for the cuff, collar, and cape. I backed the lace with red, but stopped there. Since I liked the delicate lines of the drawing, I did not want to overpower them with too much texture and tone.

The first addition was the gold and white lace headdress. That didn't detract from the drawing; as a matter of fact, it accentuated the lines of the face. I decided to use some more paper—but only pastels. The buttons, lavender sleeves, skirt bows, and bright pink shoes were added. I placed red bows on the left sleeve, skirt, and shoes. The red dots in the sleeves, as well as the colors of the wall and floor, were painted.

One of the more successful things about "Court Dwarf, Seated" is the way collage helps to give the illusion of a seated figure. The broken line of lavender bows and the three colored circles beneath the left hand seem to outline the bent knees beneath the dress.

When we removed the glass to photograph "Court Dwarf" for this book, I had the impulse to add more to it. This is an example of my belief that a picture is never really finished. It simply stops at a good place. You often see a picture you did some years before, and you wish you could add to it. Now the un-adorned right sleeve struck me as needing more. I added some bows of a red-orange paper a few shades lighter than the red I'd already used. This was to maintain the illusion of the arm being slightly turned away. I also set two small buttons of it on the other sleeve, trailed some down the skirt from the cape, sprinkled two more on the front of the skirt, and finally placed one on each shoe.

COURT DWARF, SEATED

The additional color diminished the importance of the treatment of the head. You will notice, when working with color, that each new application changes the focus of the composition. I started by giving the lady earrings and went on to encircle her head with a halo of buttons and bows cut from the newly introduced color. I also used a half-moon of it to define more perfectly the left side of the collar.

"Flowers with Wallpaper" (Frontispiece) is not related to my Elizabethan collages, but the technique I used is very similar. I began it on a 22-inch-square gesso. I first laid out my major collage area. I cut the bowl out of purple gift wrapping paper and then created the flowers by mounting concentric circles of red, orange, bright pink, and magenta. I decorated the arrangement with green paper leaves. The result was a bouquet of large, overblown roses.

FLOWERS WITH WALLPAPER

The next step was to decide how much additional collage there would be: I wanted to establish that before starting to draw. A white lace place mat defined the table. The tray was made by framing a piece of paper lace in a gold paper oval. The decoupage of the pansy with the child's head came from an old print. I backed it with a circle of lavender and framed it in a gold paper frame.

I was ready to start drawing. The first thing I did was heighten the border of the place mat with a rapid series of frilly pen and ink lines that repeated its lace. I worked freely and rapidly, so that the natural momentum of collage would not be lost.

The wallpaper was a suggestion of a fruit print. When I got to the flowers, I felt they needed more fullness, so I drew in leaves. Without color, they were lost in the background. I painted them with two shades of green acrylic. If this didn't work, I could always paste over with colored paper.

The interesting thing to me about "Flowers with Wallpaper" is the color combinations of the various shades of orange red on cyclamen red on magenta, which were used in the roses. They make a strong contrast to the lacy wallpaper background, each element holding its own in a satisfying balance.

"The Headdress" (page 87), which measures 29 by 22 inches, was done entirely on clay paper mounted on cardboard. I began by drawing the face, which I outlined in a broad circle of yellow paper for the ruff. Over this I placed a smaller circle of orange paper and I then applied three layers of white paper lace cut from mats with different patterns. I embroidered with silver crosses also cut from a paper place mat, added layers of colored paper intermingled with silver, white, and gold paper lace, and highlighted with jewels also cut from the colored paper. I sketched abstract swirls of ink muted by shadow-lines drawn with a beige marker. By filigreeing the ruff and headdress with the ink, I heightened the not inconsiderable opulence they already had. Aside from the collage, the only color was a delicate application of blue, green, and violet acrylic spots to the background, gown, ruff, and eyes.

"The Headdress" is one of my favorite collages. It is gay and sad and has a shimmering brilliance that gives the illusion of trembling motion. In fact, my whole family enjoys it so much that we inevitably find ourselves taking it with us to enhance our summer house and bringing it back again to the city when the children start school again.

MOVING ON

You have already made a simple collage, and I have described how a number of my collages were developed. Some of them may look very complicated, but once you can do a simple collage, it is only a matter of using your sense of fun and adventure to branch out to more elaborate ones. I would like to show you, step-by-step, how easy it is: you can look over my shoulder as I do it.

1.   First comes the backing: I chose a square gesso board. Over part of it I spread a piece of fabric I wanted to use for the background, and I left a healthy margin beyond the edges of the board.

I did this as a present for my husband from our sons and used a photograph he had taken of the boys. Portraits are a good inspiration, because they will immediately summon to mind elements that are uniquely personal. I hope you will want to try one yourself. When you have collected everything you think you might want to use, you are ready to begin.

2.   Next, I ironed the fabric down to remove any wrinkles and fold marks.

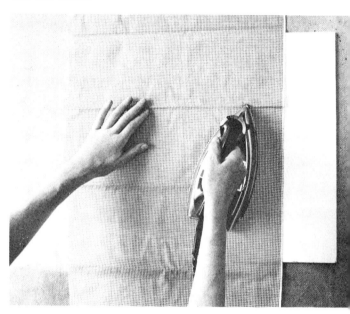

3.   I turned over the backing board and fabric and sprayed glue on the margin fabric. By using this method, I avoid the possibility of staining the background fabric— the glue goes only on the part that is behind the board.

4.   Pulling the fabric firmly and evenly to keep the front smooth, I pressed each margin down on the back of the board so that the fabric would be held securely in place.

5. *Repeating the process with a smaller piece of another fabric to cover another board. A ribbon of board was left showing.*

6. *Cutting a length of a third checked fabric to use as a strip along the bottom of the composition. If you want a clean edge, you must cut evenly, rather than shredding.*

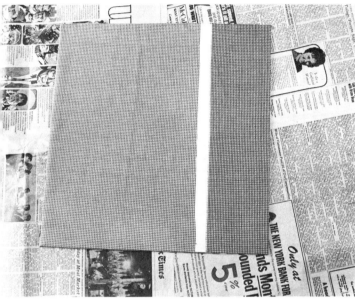

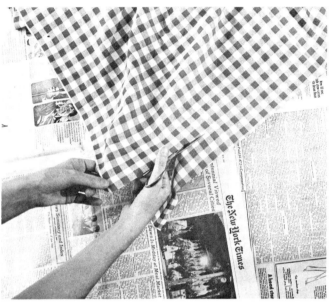

7. *When the three fabrics were in place, I decided that I didn't like the strip of bare white gesso, so I covered it with a length of ribbon. Whether or not you cover the entire background, or paint in portions of it, or use one, two, or even different fabrics for the backing will depend on your reaction to the specific combinations you make. Let your collage develop as you go along.*

8. *Trimming a length of lace for a border.*

9. I placed the lace along the edge of the picture. The backing was complete, at least for the time being.

10. I silhouetted a photograph of my two young sons, Carter and Anderson.

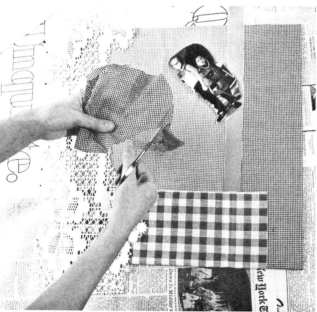

11. Then I cut out a small piece of one of the background fabrics, using the shredding technique.

12. I mounted the photograph on the piece of fabric and placed the piece on the contrasting background fabric.

. To make a frame for the photograph, I
ose an ordinary paper lace heart-shaped doily
d removed the center.

14. Now I reassembled the elements that were to go with
the photograph. I put the shredded fabric on one
heart-shaped doily and placed the "frame" on top; the
photograph became the fourth layer.

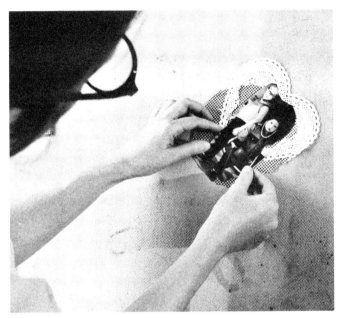

. I tried the portrait in various
mpositions with relation to the whole.

16. Finally, I hit on one position that I liked.

17. Next, I began to shred bits of other fabric to be assembled into a bouquet.

18. I built up the bouquet, scrambling the pieces until it looked right.

19. I checked the relationship between the main elements— fabric, lace, photograph, and bouquet, and shifted things a little.

20. As I moved the elements about, I added to the bouquet; at last, the whole seemed right.

I decided to make a tray to hold bits of memorabilia, d for this I cut out a circle of aluminum foil.

22. I found the right place for the tray, and on it arranged a photograph of my husband and a fragment of an article he wrote. To these I added a paper circle and a decoupage flower.

. Since this collage was a portrait of Carter and Anderson, wrote their names on some strips of paper and sitioned them on the composition.

24. The elements were ready to paste down—or just about. Since I wait till the very last minute to paste, I can take a good long look at the final arrangement.

25. Finally I was ready to paste. All the elements had fallen into place so that they felt right. Then, one by one, I removed the pieces and place them on my work area above the picture in approximately the same position as they had been in on the gesso board. This helps in returning them to their exact place after gluing.

26. I took an embroidery of my name, cut out from a handkerchief, and added it to the composition.

COLLAGE AND VARIATIONS

I have said several times that there are countless ways to arrange the elements in a collage
and the only rule for deciding which is right is what pleases your eye. I chose
the elements pictured below to demonstrate this. The subject is a Victorian nosegay.

1. From the bold floral fabric, I cut out some of the flowers.

2. I trimmed them so that just a suggestion of the background remained.

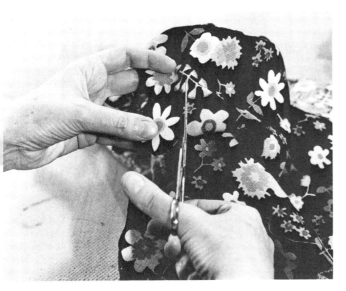

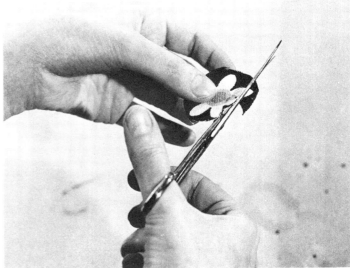

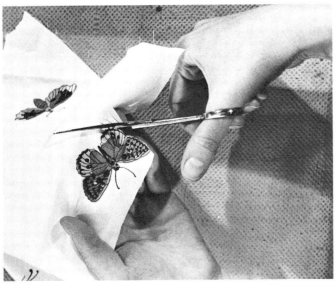

3. Using decoupage, I cut out a butterfly.

4. The first elements arranged on a gesso board covered with fabric.

5. I backed a circular paper lace mat with aluminum foil to make the outside of the bouquet.

6. The outside of the bouquet on the backing board.

7. These strips of flowers are usually available in paper stores and shops that specialize in gift wrappings; decoupage photographs of flowers could also be used.

8. I cut the strips into several pieces and snipped away the excess background.

9. *The flowers arranged in the center of the bouquet.*

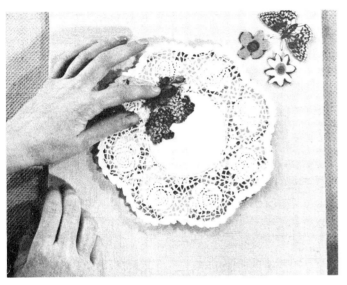

10. *I cut out some greenery in the same way as the flowers.*

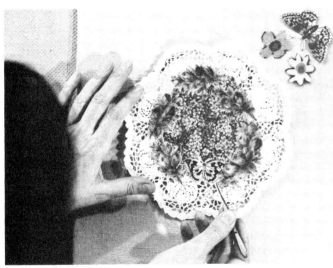

11. *When the flowers were surrounded with the greenery, and the bouquet was decorated with a butterfly, I shifted the elements around slightly until I was satisfied. (Note that I used a tweezers to move the pieces; this is a good way to work with very delicate objects clustered in a small area.)*

12. *Finally, I was ready to paste each element down.*

Above is the finished collage composed of the elements pictured on page 102. Opposite, and on pages 108 and 109, you can see three other versions I made with the same basic component parts. Many more could have developed: if you took the same elements, you could make four *different* collages, each bearing your own personal touch. I trust that's exactly what you will do now that you have seen how it's done. So set about it. Let yourself go. And have a good time. That's what it's all about, isn't it?

IN CONCLUSION

If you're going to do collage, approach it with a sense of discovery. Keep an open mind and be receptive to the things around you. In the beginning, don't *think* about it. *Do* it. As William C. Seitz, a museum curator, has written in one of his books, "No mode of creation is more direct or naturally arrived at than the accumulation and agglomeration of materials found close at hand." The artist acts spontaneously, and this spontaneity is the key to collage.

Start reacting to things *you* love. Start with one object—for me it happened to be lace—and from there let your imagination go. For one can almost define collage as the relatedness of unrelated things. It is combining something as delicate as Brussels lace with the sturdy freshness of gingham, and then discovering objects that unexpectedly relate to each fabric, and putting them all together so that each element exists in a new way. The more you develop your inner response to things, the more your imagination will grow, and out of this you will eventually arrive at your own personal style.

A friend of mine once moaned as she looked at a collage I had just finished, "But you have so much imagination! *I* wouldn't know where to begin!"

"Hold on a minute," I said. "What's your favorite color?"

She looked blank, then blinked and told me, "Blue, I guess."

"Lovely. Now, what is blue?"

"Well," she faltered, "the sky, and . . ."

"Don't think," I prodded, "just react. Go on, sky and what else?"

"Some pretty china I have, white with blue forget-me-nots—oh, and that cotton I'm making Kate's dress out of. It has blue flowers on it."

"Perfect," I said. "Use what's left over for the background of your first collage."

"Oh, I never thought of that!" She sounded excited. "And then those stamps left over from David's stamp collecting phase—just lying there in a drawer . . ."

She had no imagination? She had started with a very simple thing, her favorite color. A color she responded to. That in itself is imagination, because it evoked certain images completely personal to her and no one else. Imagination is there in all of us if we only trust ourselves. Once we do, it grows and becomes more and more uniquely our own. We must not be afraid. One of the great things about doing a collage is that no one has to see it until you want them to. It's not like getting up on a stage and performing. You're in control, and if it's not successful the first time, you simply keep experimenting until you're ready to let your family and friends see it. And even then, if they don't like it, you will—or at least you'll like something about it, if you have arrived at wanting to share it with others in the first place. Take that one thing about it you do like and use it as a springboard to go on. Your taste and style will continue to develop, and you will give yourself and the people you love a glimpse of your own unique reaction to all that is joyous and good, for collage is built out of joy and enthusiasm. Don't worry about whether or not you are an artist. It's for you to do what you must do; leave it to others to decide whether it's art or not. Whether you are an artist or not, you will find great satisfaction in trying to set down the truth of your reactions to that which you consider beautiful. You will have given it form and permanence, and that will enrich your life and the lives of those you love.

INDEX